BANDIT: AN OUTLAW FOR GOD

by

Donnie Carroll Lothridge

RoseDog Books

PITTSBURGH, PENNSYLVANIA 15238

RoseDog Books
585 Alpha Drive, Suite 103
Pittsburgh, PA 15238
Visit our website at *www.rosedogbookstore.com*

ISBN: 979-8-88527-558-3
eISBN: 979-8-88527-608-5

INTRODUCTION

Autobiography by Donnie Lothridge.

Good morning Tara. I was taught at college. To always write a letter three times before sending it. So now I am rewriting my Autobiography.

There are a lot of things in every parents life. That they wish they could have explained. Or changed and did not. And I have lived a life that is not normal.

And you are a beautiful woman now. And married to an outstanding man. That is a Christian. And that makes your Mom and I very happy.

And I pray that God. The Father, the Son, and the Holy Ghost. Keeps own reviling themselves. In a way that cannot be mistaken for the Beast.

Tara we are so Blessed to be borne in the United States of American. Were our Constitution was written by God fearing people. And our country was formed on Christianity. Because of this we are Blessed. And every country in the world has looked to us.

And I consider myself to be a true patriot. For my God, my Country, my Family, and my State. There is no greater God than the one we serve. Because of that, there is no greater Country. Than the one we live in. Our Family is full of Love. And our State is Blessed. With water, fields, and connected to an ocean.

And this is also a road map for our Government when they view my Halo. Or Beast as it is known in the Bible.

With Love from your Dad, Donnie Carroll Lothridge.

CHAPTER 1

Autobiography by Donnie Lothridge

Born September 24, 1963. As I look back into the past. At the pages of my life. And the corse God set me own. Unlike most people I have never had a clear view. Of were I was going in life. But what if?

I remember driving my dad crazy with that one question. What If? One night while he and I lay in a field. Looking at the stars, and listening to the nighttime animals. Owls , whippoorwills and frogs.

He spoke up and said, I have it. I asked, you have what? He said,that what if. You are always saying. I laughed and said, lets hear what you have. Then he said, if a frog had wings. Then he would not bump his ass every time he hopped. We laughed and laughed. That has stuck with me all my life. Did Jesus Christ walk through walls in a physical body? What if?

The Bible teaches us we were in Jesus Christ. Before the world was ever created. What if I could remember that? What if on every page of the Bible? God is saying you were here. Now don't go getting crazy on me. I was in Jesus Christ, and He was there.

What if I could remember being in Heaven, before I was born? Running and playing in the giant hallways. Surrounded by the brightness of God. And right in the middle of a perfect slide. Making a turn, to run down another hallway. God calls! Now I never got to finish my turn. And I am with God.

God said, there is a couple on earth. And they are wanting to have a son. That's when I said, I have everything here. And I do not want to leave. God said you can not develop here. Your personality, and a sense of humor. To make choices.

I asked, but Father what if I do not make it back? Then God said, not to worry, son you will be back.

Then as a tiny speck of light, I entered my moms stomach. I talked with God, and asked, when I could come back home? His answer was, not yet.

I could not believe God would send me here. But it had really happened. Yep. What if.

When I came into the world. I remember watching Angels going back and forth. Sometimes there would be three or four together. We would talk about Heaven stuff. And Gods universal power. That causes all living things to grow. And His great Love for all His creations. As we talked about animals. On Earth and in Heaven. The Unicorn, and the Dragon, the Lion and the Lamb.

Some of the Angels would come and stay for a little while. And then when those left, others would show up.

One night a Dragon showed up.

The Angels that were talking to me. Started talking to the Dragon. Then they told me the Dragon was to stay with me. For a little while. That's when they walked over to the Dragon. Patted him on the neck, and left.

The Dragon and I talked, as he was with me for a few days. One day he said, come up here. We lived in an old plantation house. That was two stories tall. And the Dragon was taller than that. It had eight foot tall windows in it. And sixteen foot sealing. With the rooftop, sixteen at the peak.

So when the Dragon said, come up here. I was lifted from my bed, and sat on his back. And passing through solid objects did not seem to be a problem. As he asked, now that was not bad was it? I said, no it was not.

He said, there is something I want to show you, so hold on. Then he took flight with me on his back. We went higher and higher. Until the earth looked like a golf ball. I could feel the power of my Father pulling me. As we drew near His planet. The Dragon asked me? Do you know who lives here? I said, God my Father lives here. The Dragon laughed and said, that is right, and do not ever forget it. I said, I will not.

Then we turned around, and started back to earth. We talked about God on the way back to earth. But I have forgotten what we said. As we came close to the earth. We circled it twice. Thats when I patted the Dragon on the neck. And asked if we could go around the earth one more time. Laughing he said, of course, hold on. We went around the earth one more time. Before going back toward were I lived. As I sat on the Dragon's back I tried to imagine, what life would be like. But all I could think about was going home. To be with my Father again. Then the Dragon said, it's time for you to be put back into your bed. He stayed with me for a few more days.

When the Angels showed up, they talked to the Dragon and I. From what I can remember the Angels, were not happy with the Dragon. I always thought it was because he took me back to God's planet. But I could be wrong. The Dragon was sad, and it made me sad to. The Dragon stayed with me, for a few more days. But never spoke another word. And when he left, the Angels left to. And I was all alone. What I have written is all true. And recorded on this Beast thing. Because I lived it. What If.

CHAPTER 2

I remember being very little, and growing up in a very large house. It was known as the Plantation home. The farmer that sold it to us, storied hay in it. It was built by slaves we were told. And they hauled the bricks from Charleston South Carolina. All this was done by horse and wagon. It was a house with a violet past. I can still remember the blood stains on the wall. That were in my bed room, that would not go away. At times you could hear people talking, and doors slamming. There were two sets of stairs in the house. And I would set and watch as the bottom step, would give in and creak. And I would watch it, as it would go all the way to the top of the stairs. And after a few moments it would start at the top, and come back down. As the spirits would move in the house. And I remember my mom going through the house. Check to see what doors were open or closed. But know matter how hot it was outside. There was always a cool soft breeze blowing in the house.

I played inside the house most of the time. But when you live in a house that large. You do not have to go outside. And my mom was always inventing new games. So I was never bored. I would go outside sometimes to play in the dirt. I remember asking God why I was here. And how long I would have to be here. Then I would say, these people don't even like me. I remember constantly searching. And looking, wondering how long. And what was life all about.

I liked to set in the big eight foot windows. And feel the warmth of the sun on my back. As I would look at the sun rays coming past me. Watching the dust dancing in the sun light.

Right down the road from us was a house. That did not look like the rest of the houses. And from setting in the window in my bedroom. I could see it clearly. That morning in early spring. I could see cars and trucks parking there. And people going inside. And I had one of those let's get mom-a moments. So I ran through the house calling her. And looking for her. When I found her, she was setting at her sewing machine. I grabbed her by the hand. Saying, come and see there are people across the road. As I pulled her through the house, she was laughing. Saying Donnie Carroll what is it. I said look there are people over there. Then at almost a whisper, I asked, what are they doing. She started laughing and said, Donnie that is a Church. And those people are going inside to learn about God. I said, I wish I could go learn about God. She said you can, but right now you are too little. But one day you will be big enough, to learn about God our Father. Jesus Christ, Gods Son, and the Holy Spirit. I said mom that is a lot. She said, it is but you are growing up fast. So before you know it you will be big enough. Then she said, those songs you heard me singing. I said, yes mam. She said, they are all about God. I did sing on the radio, for the Church of the Nazarene. My mom would sing Gospel songs all day long. And it was so nice hearing her.

One summer I was playing outside. I asked mom if I could start playing under the porch. To get out of the sun. She said it would be fine with her. So the next morning after breakfast I took my toys and went under the porch. I had Tonka toys the metal ones. A dump truck, a motor grater, and a track hoe. I had been playing under the porch for a few days.

Under the porch there was a sunken place. And it was a good place to push dirt. And my mom could come out on the porch, and check on me.

One morning before lunch, I was playing under the porch. When I looked up, there stood a little black boy and girl. She was older than he was. I would say that they were six and nine years old. She had an old time dress on. And he was wearing cover alls. I asked, if they would like to play. But she said, no thank you. I told them my name was Donnie. Then I asked, what was there names? She told me but I have forgotten. She said they could not play there. I asked her why not? She was the only one that ever spoke. He never did. I looked down at my bull dozer. And the dirt I had been pushing. And when I looked up, they were both gone.

All of a sudden, I felt one of those let's get mom-a moments. Really bad coming on. I was kicking up dust coming out from underneath the porch. As I ran into the house yelling mom-a and crying. After she held me for a little while, I calmed down. And then I told her what had happened. And she got all upset. Then she said, you will play in the house for the rest of the day. I asked,what about my toys? She said, your dad will pick them up when he gets home. I said yes mam.

My dad picked up my toys from under the porch. He said, he did not see any thing. But being under the porch, made the hair stand up, on the back of his neck. And it also give him the woollies.

Now my dad was X~military. Trained to be a sniper. And his weapon was a B.A.R. It stands for Browning Automatic Repeating Rifle. He was given iron crosses for marksman.

And he was a super cool dad, that loved to farmer.

One day as my dad was planting peanuts, and watching me. I got tired of playing in the yard. So I was watching him as he finished with a row. As he started back down the next row. Dropping the peanuts he was planting. I started crawling behind him. Picked up the peanuts he had dropped, and eating them. I almost made it a full row before he caught me. His face changed expressions three times. Before he decided what action to take.

The first words that came out of his mouth were. Thank God I did not put any poison on these seed. And then it was boy, what do you think you are doing? And then it turned into laughter. As he said, how do you think we are going to grow these peanuts. If you keep eating the seeds? Then he said, you need to stay in the yard and play. While I plant these seeds. I said yes sir.

Even though I was a child, and it's still funny to look back on. It is also scriptural. And it can be looked at in our life.

No I did not get in trouble with dad,for eating the seeds. But I sure did think I was going to. As I heard him say! I can see right now, I am going to have to cut me a switch, with this one. (What If?)

A few months later as I slept in my bed. The black girl and boy showed back up. But I could not remember there names. And it felt kinda like l was asleep, but I was not asleep. So I started calling them the spookies.

The girl said, come with us Donnie we have something to show you. I said o.k. Now to the best of my knowledge this was my first out of body experience. But it was definitely not my last. So I left my body and went with them. I looked back and seen my body laying in the bed. We went through the wall of the house. And as I followed them she said, come on we don't have much time. So we started moving faster. We went across the yards and road. And down the Church driveway. We circled the Church twice. Then went through the wall at the back of the church. Through were the people sat at. And up through the roof, were we all three sat on the cross. And we looked toward the highway, across the graveyard. This is what we wanted to show you, the girl said. As we looked into the graveyard. We could see the people that had died.

And they were reenacting the last few moments of their lives. And then there deaths. But only those that were traumatized did I see. Car wrecks, Shootings, Hangings, and Suicides. But there was only one they wanted to show me. The girl said, look this is what we want to show you.

It was an old carriage pulled by two horses. It was very stylish, and had two lanterns on the front of it.

Now there was no more graveyard. Just us watching this reenactment at the house we were living in.

There was a man, that was very well dressed, that would come out of the house. He walk across the porch and down the steps. He would walk to the fence that surrounded the house. As he opened the gate, the carriage would pull up. He would take off his top hat, and open the door to the carriage. A beautiful woman in a long dress, would reach out to him. He would take her by the hand, and help her out of the carriage. He would put his top hat back on and close the carriage door. Then he would close the gate to the fence, that surrounded the house. He would take the beautiful woman by the arm, and they would walk into the house. The door would close. In a few minutes there would be multiple flashes. Like gun shots without any sound.

Then we would be back, setting on the cross again. We would look at each other. Then at the grave yard. Were we were watching the same thing over and over.

After we had watched it four our five times. She spoke up and said, we have to go back now Donnie, we are out of time.

So we left from setting on the Cross, that was on top of the Church. Came back down the driveway. Crossing the road and the yards. We went through the side of the house. And we all stopped. Just floating, looking at me laying in the bed.

She spoke and said, you have to go back now. When she spoke that. I went over to my body, and lay down into it. My body was very cold, and I was not breathing. But as soon as I lay into my body, I started breathing again.

As I awoke the next morning. Thinking of the things that had happened. I wondered, how long I was gone from my body? And was I dead the whole time? The spookies were working in a time frame. And I seemed to be absent from my body a long time. My next question to myself was. How long can a person stay in this realm, before there is no returning to the body?

Now the Bible teaches us, to be absent from the body, is to be present with the Lord. And the Lord said, if you believed Him, you would follow Him. And not only the things He done. Would we be able to do, but greater things.

Now we as Christians know that out of our bodies, flows a river of living water. As the Holy Ghost flows through us. And that comes from our relationship. With God the Father, God the Son, and God the Holy Ghost. But it is an overflow of what the Godhead is poring into us.

Did Jesus Christ walk through walls in a physical body? (What If?) So what will happen when I step out of this body? Will I feel robbed, cheated, or fulfilled. Has it been my life, or Jesus Christ living through me. John the Baptist said it best. Jesus Christ must increase, and I must decrease. The day and time of my departure from this earth. Are written down by God. Just like all of us.

I grew up in the Vietnam era. And it was a very sad time. It seemed like I was going to a funeral every week. Death surrounded me, and I was picking up on there spirits. And I was talking to them. Most of them were very angry. And felt they had been cheated in life. But some were at peace. My mom had me a suit, and a hat. One day as we came back from a funeral. Of one of my cousins, that had stepped on a mine. And was killed instantly.

He was talking to me at his grave. Saying that it was not fare, or right that he should die that way. And that he was cheated of life. Without any warning.

When we arrived back home, I was still thinking about what he had said. When my mom said, take your suit off Donnie, and I will hang it up for you. I looked at her being a little kid and said. Why mom why? Why hang it up? I will just be drug to another funeral next week. And I will have to listen to another dead person. This family is getting smaller and smaller. Between car wrecks and the war. That's when I stopped and said, yes mam. And dad had to go by himself, to the family funerals for the next few months. Mom and I would stay at home and talk. But I could not explain how I was communicating with dead people.

Every time I have talked to the dead. There words, or sounds will not go away for sometime.

A few days later my mom went into town. And left me at home with dad. He stayed close to me and we talked about God. As he was trying to figure out what was up with me. I did not have much to say. So he turned on the T.V. He and I started watching the Olympic Games. Bobsled was on, and it was interesting. But in a little while I lost interest. And started playing with my toys. Running around the room. When all of a sudden I hit a wall. But there was nothing there. That's when the anger of those dead people rose up inside of me. And I asked why? Why God did those people have to die, without any warning? Why didn't you send someone to warn them? That's when my spirit changed inside me. And I was hit with a charge I could not explain. And a voice spoke to me I could feel. All over, and through my body. He said, Donnie that would be a good job for you. It was my Father. I stood still for a moment, while the power of God ran all over me. I was standing in front of my dad, but to his left. So he was watching me. And asked what was that. I turned from him and tried to play. With the power from God running all over me. But he stopped me and said, I asked you a question? I said, yes sir, but I can not answer it. He said try to explain to me what just happened? My only answer was, I can not. I do not know how. I felt like I was already in trouble for talking to dead people. Then I looked up at the sealing and said. Father these adopted parents just don't get it. I always thought God smiled. (What If?)

CHAPTER 3

This was also my last summer, before I started school. So I wanted to make the best of it. A Church from up the road had came by. And invited me to Vacation Bible School. And I had never been anywhere, up to this point in life. So between the man inviting me. And me pleading with mom. We talked her into it. After the man left, mom called me to her side.

She said, Donnie the world is not like we are. We live in our own little world. That we can control. The world outside is not like this. And people are basically mean. And now is a bad time for everyone. And I know you are starting school this year. And there is so much you have to learn.

I said, but mom I want to learn about God. She said, I want you to learn about God. And I want you to make friends.

The next week she took me to the church. I was so excited, I kept her laughing, telling her everything. As I told her we were going to make a little tool box, just like Jesus Christ had. And I was going to paint mine blue. I could not wait until the next day. And when I came out of the church, there she would be waiting on me.

I told her the man that had invited me to church. Was also a teacher, and was showing us how to put our toolbox's together. He taught us that Jesus Christ was a carpenter. That he went around building things, and fixing furniture. He also said, Jesus Christ fixed people that were broken. Just like a chair.

And mom, the lady taught us, that Jesus Christ walked on the water. And when the storm's of life raise up against us. Jesus Christ will come walking to us on the water.

My mom started laughing and said, that is right Donnie. When we are in trouble Jesus Christ will come walking to us on the water.

Now I knew who God is, but I had never heard so much about Jesus Christ. So I asked mom, what she thought about Jesus Christ? She started laughing with a glow about her. She said, Donnie I sing about Jesus Christ everyday. I said, mom you sing about God. She really started laughing then, and I thought we were going to wreck. As we stopped laughing I said, mom I really don't understand. She asked if I remember our conversations about the church? I said yes ma'am, you said I was too little.. She said, that is right, and you are still too little. But I will try to explain it so you will understand. God is a person. Jesus Christ is a person. And the Holy Spirit is a person. When we say God, we are talking about all three. When we pray, we are talking to all three. When we end our prayer in Jesus Christ's name we are sealing it by Jesus Christs' blood. She said as you grow you will learn, how it all fits together. I said mom I think I am still too little. She said as you grow up you will learn.

I asked her, mom does God ever talk to you? She said, He does. And then she was quite for a moment. As if she was in deep thought. Then she spoke and said, I believe God reaches out to all of us. And talks to all of us in different ways. The question is are they listening. As we got out of the car and walked into the house. I said, Mom I love you, and gave her a hug. And she said, I love you too, and gave me a kiss. So I started playing in the house thinking about God. And what tomorrow might be like.

The next day at church, we finished our toolbox. And I painted mine blue. I told mom they had taught us about Jesus Christ, feeding over three thousand people. With just three small fish, and a little bread. The lady teaching us said, Jesus Christ kept praying to His Father in Heaven. And breaking those fish and bread until everyone had enough to eat. My mom smiled as she always did. And said, that is right Donnie, He did.

That day back at the house, I thought about what I was learning. And the things mom had said. And thinking how it all fit together. Then I asked myself were do I fit into all of this?

Mom took me to Church the next day. And when she picked me up everything had changed. They had taught us how they arrested Jesus Christ. And tortured Him, by spitting on Him. And slapping Him, pulling out His beard. They beat Him with a whip called cat-o-nine tails. It had pieces of bone and metal put in it. So it would cut and jerk out chunks of flesh. And they made a crown from thorns, and put it on His head. Then we were taught Jesus Christ was made to carry His Cross. To a hill called Golgotha. Were they nailed Him to it. And killed Him.

As we rode down the road mom asked me if I was alright? I busted out crying thinking of how Jesus Christ was treated, and killed. I asked mom to please take me back to Church. She said I will Donnie but I think they have all gone home. And she was right.

We started back home my heart was breaking into, as I cried and cried. My mom said Donnie, I think I know what is wrong. Through the tears I said mom. I can not believe they could torture and kill Jesus Christ like that. She said, it is true Donnie, but He died for all us forever. Then I started crying again. My mom said Donnie, I think I know how to fix this. And gave me a little smile. She said it is called the Romans road to Salvation. It is the reason I sang on the radio. I said, I don't know if it can fix this mom. She smiled and said trust me. Then she said, Donnie according to Romans 10: 9-10 if we declare with our mouth, that Jesus Christ is Lord, and believe in our heart,that God raised Him from the dead. We shall be saved. I said, I believe that mom. Then she said, pray with me Donnie this little prayer of faith. Confessing all our sins to Jesus Christ. And you will be saved. I said yes mam.

Then she said repeat after me. We ask You now Jesus Christ to forgive us of all of our sins. And to come into us, and be Lord of our life. For we know and believe, You suffered under Pontius Pilot, and was crucified. Died and was buried. Resurrected on the third day. And now is seated on the right hand of God. Interceding for us. Come into me,and and be Lord of my life. In Jesus Christ name I pray. Amen! At that moment I was changed. And my tears of anger and hurt. Turned into tears of joy and peace. Knowing I was saved. For God sent His

Son into the world not to condemn it, but that through Him the world might be saved. John 3: 17 (What If?)

The Lord and I spent the rest of that Summer with each other. And the spookies would always be around. Wanting to show me different things. And I new school was coming. And it turned out to be more than just a night mare. The school had not been separated. So it was from the first grade to graduation. And from day one I was beaten up, pushed around, and bullied every day. I had no friends during that time, and it was crazy. And my mom was right, the world is a cold cruel place. And I came home crying every day.

But God and His people can be found no matter were you are. So I started leaning into God more. My dad started talking to them at school. Trying to find out what was wrong and fix the problems.

When I was in the fifth grade, my dad sold the plantation house. And we moved a few miles down the road. Our new house was not completed. So we moved into a camper my uncle owned. One evening a lightning storm came up. My mom was passing the floor, and praying. All of a sudden I walked to the door were she was standing. And said, mom I hate lightning. A bolt of lightning struck outside the camper door. Inside the camper we could feel the charge from it. And mom instantly slapped me in the mouth. Nocking me backwards. And screamed don't ever say that. Then she grabbed me in a big hug. Kissing the top of my head. She said, don't ever say that Donnie. We both were crying, as I said, yes mam.

I had achieved to having two friends by then. And he and I were totally opposite of each other. He had been through a lot of pain and suffering in hospitals. And I had not, and he was a fighter, and I was not. And he cussed, and I did not. One day at school he and I were talking. And a bully came up and started pushing me around. My friend spoke up and said. Why don't you go on somewhere else. You know he does not fight, and he is a Christian. The bully said, then when I get through kicking his ass, I am going to kick yours. My friend said, fuck yes, that is what I am talking about. I am not a Christian, and I love to fight just to see, a mother fucker like you bleed. And the bully backed down.

After the bully had left I thank my friend. He said, sooner or later, you are going to have to fight. I said, I don't know how. He said, it does not take a lot, to knock the fuck out of somebody. I said, I don't like that. And why do you have to cuss so much? He said, I get my point across. And you are going to have to start taking up for yourself. Because I am not your babysitter. We were quite for a moment. And then he started laughing and said. I almost made him piss in his pants. I said, you did and started laughing to.

As we moved into the new house. I was hit with depression. I would stand under a tree, and cry to God for hours.

But the straw that broke the camels back. Was when two teenage boys hung me out of the back of the school bus. And made me drag my feet on the road. My dad was so mad. He said, I think I will take you to school from now on. And I will see you tomorrow when you get home. I said, yes sir, and what about my shoes? He said, I will get you a new pair. So the next morning he took me to school, and dropped me off. On the school bus ride home. They started talking and laughing about what they had done to me. As we got close to the house, I could see my dad. He was standing next to the mailbox, dressed in his military fatigues. He had a hair cut and went all out. He had a shotgun in one hand, and two dead rabbits in the other. As the bus came to a stop. You could have heard a pin drop, it was so quiet. I walked to the front of the bus. But my dad told me to stop as I got close to were the driver was setting. Then my dad said, Mr. bus driver you and I are going to have us a little talk. Do you see that boy standing behind you? The bus driver said, yes sir. My dad said, well you see God gave him to me. For me to protect and raise. So what happened yesterday should have never happened. The bus driver said, I should have stopped it. My dad said, you should have done a hell of a lot more than that. Then my dad said, it is over with now. But as you and I both know. If we have to have another talk like this one. You are not going to like me very much. And afterwards neither will your parents. He adjusted the shotgun under his arm, looking at the bus driver and said. We do understand each other, right. The bus driver said yes sir, then asked if my dad was going to report him. My dad said no sir, you and have straightened this out. And you have to come by my house every day. Then my dad said, come on boy and I got off the bus. As we walked across the yard my dad put his arm around me. And said, I think that young man understands me. I said yes sir, if he missed that there is something wrong with him. Then my dad turned to me and said. Donnie there are things in life we have to do. Not because we want to, but because we have to. I said yes sir. He said, I think a good place to start, would be learning you how to survive. In the woods.

After a few days my friend said, I heard about what your dad did. I started laughing and said, that was something wasn't it. He said, there is something else I need to tell you. I said, what is that. He asked, have you ever wandered why your knuckles are so black, on your hands? I said, I have noticed that but so are yours. He said, it is because I am Native American Indian, and so are you. I said, I will have to ask my mom. But you are probably going to get me a whipping. I have tried to play cowboys and Indians. And she will not let me play that way. He said, do you see the long black hair your mom has? And how dark her skin is? She is an Indian. I said, that does not make her an Indian. He said, then let's do it this way before I go forward with this. Look at your kin people from your moms side. They are all very dark skinned. With jet black hair. I said, they are. Then he said, my Grandpa is a very important person to our people. And I asked him about you. I asked, and what did he say? He said, you are a distant cousin. I said, my mom is going to kill me. And we both started laughing. Then he said, do you think that is funny? Your Grandma on your dad's side is a Horn. And that is Indian to. Then we started laughing again. I said, now that is funny. He said, but I am not laughing. And one day I will take you to meet my Grandpa. And he will tell you what I have. I said, thank you I will ask my mom. And I did.

She told me something's from her childhood. And she told me it was true, from both sides of the family. So I asked her, can we hide who we are. And she said no, we can not hide who we are. Even though we are set apart. We are still Citizens of the United States of American. And I want you to grow up that way. Your friend is almost full blooded Indian. And you are probably half. But just try to live life happy, and full of love. That is all that I am saying. I said, yes mam. I never told anyone what my mom and I talked about that day.

The next day at school my friend asked me, if I had talked to my mom. I said, yes I did, and she whipped my ass. His face dropped for a moment in disbelief. And I could not help it, I busted out laughing. He said, you are such a lier. And we both started laughing. Then I said, you are right. My Grandma from both sides have Indian in them. I said, but that does not change who we are. He said, no but one day we will meet my Grandpa. And he will confirm what I said. I said, yes I would like to meet him.

CHAPTER 4

June 14, 2021
Autobiography by Donnie Lothridge

I believe God always sends someone. Into our lives, and then it is up to us. As to what happens, sometimes it is for the better. And sometimes it is for the worst. My friend and I were going to church one morning. And we both had caught a mason jar full of white headed bumblebees. And decided to take them with us to Church. As we were in Sunday School class he said. I am going to turn my bumblebees loose. I said, do not do that, if you do everyone will have to leave the Church. He smiled and said, I know. I said, we are going to get in trouble. He said, I know. I looked back and he had the lid of the jar, just setting on the top of it. I said don't do it. He said smiling, as he slung them bees out of the jar. And hollered oh hell they got loose. We cleared that Church. On the way back home I told him. You know God wrote that down. He said, I never thought about it that way. We both started laughing. And then I said, you know normally when I laugh this hard. It is followed by an ass whipping. He said, I never thought about that either. And we laughed some more. Now our parents got a visit from the preacher. And I thought I was going to get whipped by both of them. After the preacher left.

My mom and dad set me in-front of them. And my mom looked at my dad and said, that is your boy. As she was trying to keep a straight face. My dad with a half grin on his face said. Now you know he is half yours. And then they started laughing. As my dad asked, how did the people act when those bees got loose. I said, it was like we had set the place on fire. There were people screaming and running swatting bees.

My mom was laughing so hard. She made me stop telling the story so she could go and pee. She said, she had almost wet her pants. When she came back into the room. She said, I am alright now let's start again. My dad asked, then what did y'all do? I said, After the shock of watching people run over each other, trying to get out of the door. We got in the line screaming run, run the bees got lose. And they started laughing again. Then my dad said, those were white headed bumblebees. I said yes sir. None of them had a stinger. Then my mom and dad stopped laughing. And my dad said, well there is no more Church for you. And I said, but dad. Mom spoke up and said, and you can not see your friend for two days. I said, but mom. Then she said one day. Then she changed it to a half a day. My dad laughing said, you had better go outside son before we change our mind. On the way out the door I heard my dad tell my mom. I see more of you in him every day. She started laughing and said, that was all of you there. And I heard them both laughing.

When I seen my friend again he asked me. Tell me did you get your ass whipped. I said, no but I should have. Then I asked, how about you. He said, hell no my dad thought it was funny. I said mine to. Then I asked, why is it every time I think I am going to get a whipping I don't. And when I don't think I am going to get a whipping I do. Then he said, somethings you did were wrong and you will never do them again. For those things you will not get a whipping for. But the things you do knowing they are wrong. That is what you get a whipping for. Then I said, you have a really cool dad. He said I know. Then he said, we are going to have to find something to get a whipping for. I asked him are you crazy? And he said, yes I am. And we both started laughed.

So over the Summer our friendship grew. Now we had entered the six grade. And my tormentors had not forgotten a thing. But some of them had backed off because of my friend.

There whose one boy at school that kept trying his best to start a fight with me. My friend said, now there is your trouble. Your going to have to kick his ass, or he is going to kick yours. I asked my friend, why do people have to be so mean? He said, it is the way things are. Then he said, welcome to the real world Donnie. Later that day we were switching class room's. And as we walked outside he jumped me. My body ran hot with blood and fear. As I turned lose on the boy swigging wild. I had beat him to the ground. Before I realized it, and it was over.

My friend said, now that should make you feel better. I said, it does not make me feel better. It only proved there is something else living inside of me. He started laughing and said, I am glad you finally let it out. What, that my fear turned into anger. He said, if that is what you want to call it. He said, Donnie people are angry now because of the war. I said, believe me I have talked to enough dead people. That have died in this war to know that. He started looking hard at me and said. You are a very strange person Donnie. I started laughing and asked him? If he would like for us to spend the night in the Plantation House? His face turned into a state of shock. As he said, fuck you and them spookies. He had tried to sleep over a couple of nights. But around ten o'clock at night. The spirits would start moving around. Slamming doors and talking, and he would go back to his house.

I started laughing and said, them spookies do not like you. He started laughing to. As he said, fuck them spookies. I said, they love me. Jokingly I asked, why don't the spookies like you? He said laughing, I am not talking to you Donnie.

The rest of the year at school went pretty well. With my dad taking me to school. And working with me on the weekends. But depression was slowly working on me. And Satan was giving me suicidal thoughts. Operating in the spiritual realm I knew self harm, was as not the answer.

At the new house there was a tree that I would stand under and cry out to God. Asking God for guidance and protection. And seeking His face. Knowing my life had now became a battle ground for good and evil. But why I asked, dose everyone go through this? Where is my life going? And how do I get around this? Or will I have to go through it? Then I would cry out to God and say, I can do nothing own my own, but through You, I can do all things. I run into You God, saying I am going to need You.

Now I was always scared of my dad, even though all of our relatives loved him. And confided in him. My dad was an outside person who loved nature, camping, and fishing. Love and respect flowed through him, and he was a people person.

He loved to tell me, if you think you have it bad Donnie look around you. There are a lot of people struggling in life. That understands the world does not owe them a thing. I would always say yes sir. Knowing what he was going to say next. As he would say, if you can't see that son. We can ride to the hospital, and as we walk down the hallways. Ask your self what circumstances put them there. Was it something they done, or not. Will they walk out of there, or not.

And dad always tried to show me God, in everything. And like most of us, that have lived for any length of time. He had seen the good, the bad, and the ugly. And he loved this country. As he started training me basic survival skills, he would fall back on his military training. And tell me stories of when he was in the service. He would always say to me, everything has a spirit to it. And nature as beautiful as it is, will kill you if you do not respect it. And something as simple as a piece of plastic can save your life. I would always laugh and say yes sir. And as we would walk through the woods, he was always eating something he had found. I would always say one day your going to eat something that is going to kill you. And he would laugh and say, no son I know what I am eating. And if you ever get lost in the woods. When they find you, or you come walking out of the woods. I want you to be very much alive. And I would say yes sir.

Now my concentration was on the beauty of the Lord. And my dad was working on me, getting me in top physical condition.

My dad tried to give me a variety of things to keep me busy. He bought me a pony. That I practically lived on. And we started going to Church. He tried to keep me super busy, to pull me out of my depression. And we would talk often about God. It had been a long summer and I had hoped this year, the seventh grade at school would be different.

As the next school year started some friends from the church said they would take me home. I had not been taken home by them but a few days when the power of God hit me. As we pulled into a store I said. You know I am going to quit school. As I am looking into the Spirit realm. There daughter sitting in the front seat says. Donnie you really should not quit, that is your future. I said, I do want to quit and I am. People are mean, and I do not fit in. And looking ahead I can not see me graduating. But you are very smart and that makes the difference. She said something else while I was looking into the future. And it changed what I was looking at, in the Spirit realm.

And I said did you know that in your senior year you will have a car wreck and be killed. Her mom asked, how I knew this. I told her, I just do.

Her and a friend, her senior year was driving home from a football game. When they lost control of the car and wrecked. Both girls were killed.

I looked forward to the day when she and I can talk, and walk down the golden streets in Heaven. Looking at the beauty of our Father's house! All of our days here on earth are written down. And we will not live past the second, God has appointed for us to be taken home. (What If?)

Not long after that my friend showed up at our new house. He said, the people that had bought the Old Plantation House, had gone out of town. And had asked him if he would feed and water the animals, while they were gone. And he said he would. So he asked my mom, if I could ride with him to take care of the animals. She said, that would be good with her. So I hugged and kissed my mom, like I always did if I was going somewhere. We almost made it to his dads car, when my mom with a grin on her face. Asked, have you been driving very long? My friend froze in his tracks, as we both turned around to face my mom. He said, no mam but I am a safe driver, and my dad let's me drive. She started laughing and said, that's nice now you boys buckle up. And go straight to the house and come back. That way if something was to happen to y'all, I will know were y'all are at. We said, yes mam and got into the car. As she went back into the house.

On the way up the road I asked him, how long he had been driving? He said, I have not started driving yet. I said, you mean to tell me I am in a car with you, and you have no driving license? He said, I did not know I had to have any. We both started laughing. Then he said, look here, the reason I came and got you. Yesterday while I was feeding the animals, the spookies showed up. And I do not want any trouble from them ghost. I said, so you are saying the spookies don't like you. He said that is not what I am saying. I am saying that they like you better.

I said, well I can see were that could be a problem. Because if the spookies does not like you, then I don't like you either. He started laughing and said, I can see this was a mistake. Maybe we can sneak in, feed the animals, and leave. And they want even know we were there. I said, but I have not seen them in a long time. He said, and maybe it will be a longer time before you see them again. I said, but its the spookies.

He said, you remember what I said, and do not start any shit up here. I said yes sir, as we pulled into the driveway. Then I said, just like Santa Claws, in and out before they know it. So we walked up the steps, and onto the porch. He opened the door, and stepped into the house. And I was right behind he. As I past through the doorway, I took a good look at the way they had their furniture arranged. And it was much like we had our furniture when we owned the house.

He stopped and said, they had changed things around a little bit. They moved the kitchen into your bedroom.

Before I took another step, I looked past the cat that was asleep on the couch, and looked up the stairs. As I hollered spookies I am home, did you miss me, I want to play. My friend started fussing, as he said, I told you not to do that. You know I do not like ghost, and they scare the hell out of me. I started laughing as we walked into the kitchen. And then I stopped laughing as I was looking around at what was my bedroom. Then I said, this is nice, but I wonder what the spookies think about it. Then my friend said, this is were I ran into problems last time I was here. But then this room always did freak me out. So let's feed these animals and get the hell out of here before they show up. I started laughing again, and he asked, what was so funny.

I said the spookies are already here. Then he asked, how do you know that? I said, do you see that cat that is asleep on the couch? He said, yes. I said, know matter what happened that cat did not wake up. He said, I noticed that to. I said, and the spookies, they do not like cats. He said, Donnie don't you start your shit up in here. I said, but the spookies want to play. He said, Donnie! I said, watch this, as I raised my arm and pointed at the sleeping cat. Both eyes flew open, as the cat stared at me, bowing its back. As the hair stood up all over the cat. It hissed at me pawing, before jumping off the couch, and onto the screen door. The door came open and the cat jumped onto the porch. As we watched the walls disappear, so we could see the cat, as it ran across the yard. Jumping a fence, and running into the pine trees behind the house.

I turned and looked at my friend, that was screaming out something. But I could not hear him. So I put my hand up to my ear. And screamed back, I cannot hear you. That's when he turned from me, and started slinging dog food and water. Trying to get out of there as fast as possible. When he had finished feeding the animals, he turned to me. Trying to speak to me again and realizing, we still could not hear each other. He screamed like a woman, and I could hear that. As he ran out of what was my bedroom, into the hall area were the cat was asleep on the couch. Still screaming like a woman. And I was right behind him, telling the spookies goodbye, and that I loved them. And I was glad that we got to play and have fun. As he ran out of the house and onto the porch. He said, I will get the car, you lock the door to the house. I could hear gravel slinging from the tires, as I turned around jumping off the porch laughing. And ran to the car as he was turning it around. The car was still moving as he reached over and opened the passenger door. Hollering get in quick before the spookies get you. As I jumped into the car laughing so hard I was crying. Trying to stop from laughing because my friend was very upset.

CHAPTER 5

June 24, 2021

Autobiography by Donnie Lothridge

I kept having those bust out laughing moments, as we drove down the road not saying anything. About a mile or two down the road he pulled the car over. He said, we have to go back and find that cat. I started to speak when he said, don't talk to me. Shaking his head yes, trying to talk himself into going back. He says again, we have to go back and find that cat. Then he looks at me and asked, what the hell was that, that just happened? A smile came across my face as I said, I think they are called the spookies. He said out of all the people I could have as a friend, I picked one that talks to dead people. The smile left my face, but now he was smiling. As he started turning the car around and said, let's go find that cat. I said, we can go look for the cat, but I don't think we will ever find it. So we went back and looked for the cat, but we never found it. (What If?)

So we got back into the car and started towards my new house. There was a Black Church that was up the road from my house. And he pulled into it and stopped. Then he asked, what the hell are you Donnie? I started laughing and said, there is not a correct answer for that question. But after looking at the seriousness of my friend, I could tell play time was over. I said, I am a Christian. But other than that I am just like you are. And there is were my friend went off on me. He said, bullshit Donnie, you do not see me going around talking to dead people. In my defense I said, I do not go around talking to dead people. He said, then what the hell is the spookies, if they are not dead people? And what the hell happened to the cat? And why did I

park in the middle of a graveyard, for us to have this conversation. I must be losing my mind, get in the car we are moving. I could tell my friend was very upset, as we were riding down the road. So I said, I am just like everyone else. And I believe the spookies were killed in that house, and in the room we were in. My old bedroom. And he seemed to get better until I said, but the spookies do not like cats.

That's when he slung the car into a dirt road and slammed on breaks. As the car slid to a stop, he put it in park and said,get out. As we walked to the front of the car and leaned against it, almost setting on the hood. He asked, how can we be standing less than five feet apart. Screaming at the top of our voices and not being able to hear each other. That is not normal, can you explain it to me. I could tell my friend was starting to get upset again. Then he asked, how does a wall disappear. Then he turned and walked away from car. After about fifteen steps he stopped, and walked back to the car.

He said let's ride down to the river. As he and I got back into the car I said, the river sounds good. A place for relaxing and looking at the beauty, and power of God. I said, it will be fun, and I love the river. On the way there he started mumbling to himself. I asked, what did you say? He said, I did not say anything Donnie. Then I said, you are talking to yourself. And asked, do you talk to yourself much? He said, that is because I know who I am. And I still don't know who you are. I started laughing and said, now that is a terrible thing to say to me. As we pulled up on the bank of the river. And got out of the car.

I said, I know it is not the spookies you want to talk to me about, but God. He had another fit about the spookies, as I watched him and listened. Then I asked,are you alright now? He said, I am but I still can't get it straight in my mind. I said, do not try, it is just something that just happened. Then I changed the subject and said, let's talk about God.

That is when he said, I heard about what you said, to the girl. How she was going to die in her senior year. Is what you said, connected to the spookies or the house. I said, no it has nothing to do with the house or the spookies. What I said to the girl, was from God. And what happened to us today was from the spookies. God is life that flows through all things living. The spookies are dead, but there spirits are still here. Do not ask me why they are here, they just are. And from what they have showed me, it is because of the way they died.

Then he asked, can God change what He has shown you? I said, He can but why would He. God is the life giver and God is the life taker. Her days were written down just like ours. And God has a greater plan for her, than she could ever be given here on earth. When God takes her home, she is perfect in His eyes. We are the only ones that will have a problem with it. Because we live in an upside down world. According to the Bible we should rejoice over her death. A young beautiful woman has gone home. And has been taken by God from all this bullshit going on down here.

He could tell I was about to get cranked up. So he tried to change the subject by asking, what about the spookies? I said, now you just went from a Living God to the grave. The spookies are dead. It is true they chose to show me there world. But it is two different worlds. We live in a parallel world with the after life. And death is always present, we are only one breath away from it. But my choice in life is God. And only because of God are any of us here.

He said, I feel I need to take you back home. Your mom must be wandering where we are by now. I said yes we do not want to get into trouble with mom. So we got in the car and we drove back to the house. He asked, why is the spookies there, they are supposed to be with God? I mean they are children right? I said, they are, and we both know the age of accountability is twelve years old. Then he said Donnie, I think they might be older then twelve. And just look to be under twelve. Because we both know God does not lie. As we pulled into the driveway my mom was sweeping the carport. He said, she is worried about us, I said, she is. He said, I will see you later as I got out of the car. He waved and said goodbye to my mom, as he turned the car around and left.

As I walked up on the carport I hugged and kissed my mom. She asked if I had fun, and I said yes mam. Then I said, the spookies showed up and scared my friend. She started laughing and said, I do not miss that house. I told her how they had rearranged the front of the house. And said, I do not think the spookies like it. Then she said, that house is to big. She started laughing as I told her everything that had happened. As I finished telling her, she said, I am glad we know longer live there.

Then I asked her if she remembered when I beat a hole in the wall upstairs? I watched as the expression changed on her face, and thought, this might not have been the smartest thing to ask. She asked me if I remembered being drug down the stairs, while she was whipping my butt? I said yes mam, I had a very bad day then, but the spookies wanted me to do it. She said if you keep talking like that, and reminding me of that day. I will do it again. I said, yes mam, as I watched a smile appear back on her face. I said mom, I love you, and she said, I love you to. Then she said, I am finished out here let's go inside. I watched as she fixed a cup of coffee, and set down on the couch.

She picked her Bible up and opened it, to the page she had marked. And she almost started to laugh again, from the expression on her face. I thought now is she thinking about the spookies half scaring my friend to death. Or is she think about whipping my ass as she drug me down those steps. I thought well she is happy and that is all that counts.

The next day my friend showed back up, and asked if I could go with him again. To the Plantation House to try and find the cat that was lost the day before. My mom busted out laughing and said, that will be fine. My friend asked her if I had told her what had happened, and she said yes. And started laughing as she said you boys have fun. And be careful, you never know what the spookies might do. He said, we are not going into the house, we are just going to look for the cat. I hugged and kissed my mom, assuring her we would be careful. As we went out the door, I asked him if we were really going to look for the cat. He said, we have to find that cat before the owners of the house come back. I said, we can look, but we will not find that cat. As we pulled into the driveway I said, hello spookies, I am back. He said, you shut the hell up. I am not going through another day, of what I went through yesterday. My brain still hurts. He said, you look around the house and I will look in the edge of the woods. I said, yes sir. He and I looked for about two hours, but we never saw the cat.

When we got back into his dads car he said, let's ride to the river. I said, all right the river, I love the river. He said, there is something very important we have to talk about. And the river would be a good place. When we arrived at the river he said, I know you told the girl her future. Then he asked, who else's future can you tell? Then I asked, what do you want to know about? He asked, what about your cousin? I said let's ride around for a minute. He said, alright as we got back into the car I started looking into the Spirit realm. I said, the things I am about to say to you, you will probably not like. He said, Donnie there are a lot of things about you I do not understand. I stopped him and said, I don't understand them myself, but I am learning. And the devil has already tried to kill me, but I will answer your questions, if I can.

He said, I asked about your cousin? I said o. k. here we go. I said, my cousin will marry. They will buy a farm. They will get a divorce, she will take the children with her. Child support will eat him alive, he will come to me and we will pray. Two of the children will come back and live with him, but only for a short time. Then I stopped speaking. We set quite for a little while, then he asked what about me.

I started laughing and asked do you really want to know? He had a look on his face, that told me he was not to sure about this. That made me laugh even harder. Then I said, o.k. here we go. God will bless you. We laughed and laughed and then he asked, as our laughter slowly stopped. What about you he asked? I turned and looked out the window as I gazed into the Spirit realm. We were quite for a moment. And then I said, they will kill me, I have an appointment with Jesus Christ I can not miss. He said, that cannot be right, and it is very sad. Then I said, it is right, but I do not stay dead. God has to show me some things and then I will be back. I stayed in the Spirit realm looking for a minute, then I came back to my self. I said, let's talk about something else this is bringing me down. He said, I can not believe that you will die. I said, you better, it is going to happen. Then I looked back in Spirit realm to see how long it would be. There was a flash of light measuring the distance. Then I said don't worry it's not that close yet.

We rode around for a while but not talking, then I asked to be taken back home.

As I returned home I started thinking about the things we had talked about. And the beauty of the the Lord, and how good the sun felt on my skin. I could feel the love of God all over me, as I wondered how God was going to make it all happen. For the next few months I spent looking to God, and I was rapped. My mom said, never let your dad find it out, he will kill him and go to prison. I could feel my spirit being pulled away from God, and I did not like that. I withdrew into myself wondering what went wrong. But I was solid on the inside knowing who I am in God. I remember running thoughts over and over in my head. On how I was going to kill him and dispose of the body. But then I would start crying and say, I have to think about something else. He will get his, as I would turn it over to God. And I would go to sleep at night crying, praying to God.

My dad knew something was wrong because I stopped going anywhere. I told him you can whip my ass if you would like, but I am not going anywhere. And that was all I would tell him, so he could tell I was very upset.

My friend after about a month came back over. He said, I just heard what had happened to you. That man is going all over town talking about what he done to you. I said, yes it is true. He asked, do you mind if I visit for a little while? I said, no I do not mind, in fact I could use the company. Then I said, I guess now my dad will find out and kill him. He said, yes there is no way for your dad not to hear about it.

And said, all these nights I have thought of what I was going to do to him. Then I said, no I do not want to bring you into this. We will just see what God is going to do. Then he asked, would you like to get out of the house and go for a ride. I said no, I don't feel like going any where. I said, I just want to stay in my room and think. He said, in a case like this I think you have done enough thinking. We set quite for a moment or two, then he stood up and said, I will see you later. I said, thank you for coming by. He said, any time as he left.

I continued seeking and praying to God, looking for answers, and looking into the future.

I asked mom if she would pick me up a guitar. One of those little plastic ones, just to see if I really wanted to learn how to play one. And she did. I was setting on my pony, strumming on the guitar, singing to God. When the piece that holds all the strings together came lose. And slapped me in the face, knocking me off the pony, and onto the ground. As I shook my head getting my since back. Satan spoke up and said, do you still want to praise Him, do you still want to praise God? I jumped up grabbed my guitar and slung it across the yard. Saying, yes Satan I will praise God until the day I die. Jumped back on the pony and put him back up. I walked back into the house, gave my mom a kiss. She asked, Donnie what's wrong, and were is the guitar? I said, mom, Satan slapped me in the face with that thing, and I slung it across the yard. And it can stay there for all I care! My mom started laughing and said, that sounds like Satan.

A few nights later after crying, and thinking of where I could trap that man at. And saying my prayers, I went to sleep. Around two or three in the morning, I was wakened by a light in my room. And a stirring in my spirit. I sat up to the screaming of the man that had raped me. And watching the flames of hell over taking him. As he kept repeating over and over, do you know what they done to me. Donnie do you know what they done to me. Shrieks and screams filled my room, as he kept crying out to me. Then I said, if I had caught you, I would have done the same thing. Then he was gone, and a piece came over my room, and me. As I said, thank you Father, Son, and Holy Ghost. And I went back to sleep.

The next day my friend showed back up, he asked if I had heard what had happened. I smiled and said, no I have not heard, you know I don't get out much. He and I started laughing as he said, I guess not. Then he said, somebody killed that sick piece of shit last night. I looked at him smiling and said, really. He said, you already knew it. I said, I did. He asked how, did God tell you? I said, God showed me. Then he asked, how do you do that? You talk to God, and you talk to dead people. Is there not a wall there that keeps you on one side or the other. Then he said, let's go for a ride and we can talk about it as we ride around. I said, I will ask mom if it is o.k. Then he said, I have already asked, and she said yes. So I said, let's go. And kissed my mom on the way out the door.

As we road around he said, I am still waiting for your answer on what I asked. I said alright, you know while we are alive we are making a choice. And when we die we get our reward. Was my choice towards Heaven, or was my choice toward Hell. We also know that when we die there is a gulf between the two. Now we have made our decision in life, and we were so sure of it. God has provided us any eternity of what we have sowed. That is what we shall reap forever. He said, that did not answer my question.

I said, I am not dead yet, and there is no wall that I can tell of. But there is one question, were do I want to spend forever at? He gave me one of those silly little laughs, and said, that is the question isn't it. I said, now I have a question for you. Did Jesus Christ walk through walls in a physical body? He thought for a moment and said, yes he did, and people to. I started laughing and he asked, wasn't I right? I said, you are exactly right. Then I asked, if Jesus Christ did it, doesn't that mean I can do it to? He started laughing and said, yes I guess so. After that he took me back home, and he left. (What If?)

CHAPTER 7

June 30, 2021

Autobiography by Donnie Lothridge

We had talked about farming on my grandparents land. And after everything I went through, my mom and dad thought it would be a good idea. If I went and stayed with my grandparents for a few days. They were anointed and most days you could feel the Lord's presences from them. And after raising twelve children of their own. They had probably ran into about everything there is. I was scared of my grandpa, because I knew he meant what he said. And he stayed in the Bible reading it. The book he loved the most was Isaiah, and I remembered asking him, was that his favorite book in the Bible, and he said yes.

The first day I was there, I spent following my grandpa around. And listening to him as we walked the one hundred acre farm. We counted the cows, and looked at the corn he was growing. When we made it back to the barn, he picked up a hoe, and said, follow me boy I have a little work to do. He never called me Donnie, it was always boy. As we left the barn, we walked in a cow path to the garden. I was looking at the little butterfly's flying around the bitter weeds, and butter cup's. All of a sudden the power of God ran through me. And it was like, I could see an Angle standing at the corner of the field. My grandpa asked, are you o.k. boy? I said yes sir. He said, good then come on smiling. He opened the gate and we went into the garden, as he worked we talked. And then there was the power of God again, surging through me like before. But this time it was like I was out of my body. And it lasted for about two minutes, when I came to, I could hear my grandpa laughing. Then he said, you have it don't you boy. I said, yes sir I do have it. And smiling he said, it is a gift from God, and it will grow in you just like these tomatoes are growing. I smiled and said, yes sir.

Then his voice changed, as he said forcefully. I see you have already ran into trouble. And believe me some people ant worth killing. I said, yes sir. He said, now the only thing you have to do is settle this in God. Because if you don't this thing will haunt you. And you will hurt yourself. I asked, grandpa what if I don't know how to settle it in God. He said, believe me boy, you know how to settle it. I said, yes sir. My grandpa was looking into me, the way he did his own children. Some people call it reading you. But it was a new experience for me. To have a seer for a grandpa.

Now my grandpa said, you know boy Satan is trying to kill you. I said, yes sir I do. He said, but God is with you. And your life will not be easy. And there will be times you will walk away from God. But God will never leave you, nor will He forsake you. I said, yes sir. Then he said something that shocked me. He said, my time is very short here on earth now, and I will be leaving. To go be with my Father in Heaven. I said, yes sir I can feel that to. He said, good, good boy, as he patted me on the shoulder. He said, come on we are through here in the garden. And I want to be setting in my chair outside, reading the Bible, when the sun goes down. I said, yes sir. As he opened the Bible he said, good evening God, what will you show me today. I started laughing and so did he.

He said, when ever you open the Bible, remember you and God are going to have a talk. I said, yes sir. I sat quite after that until sun down, just looking at the beauty of the Lord.

When I went to bed that night my grandma came into the room. And tucked the covers around me, asking if I was alright? I said yes mam. Then my grandpa came in and pulled the window down just a little bit at the top. I said, thank you sir as he left.

That night as I prayed I said, now God I know there are a lot of roads that I will have to travel in this life. And on a lot of them I look to be alone. I am at peace with myself because of Your great love. But I asked now for Your protection, and that Your presence be forever with me. And I am now going to leave everything with You Father, and I am going to seal it in Jesus Christ Name. Let Your Holy Spirit Flow, because without the Three of You, I am alone. Let the Joy of the Lord come and be my strength. For Lord You are my Bright and Morning Star. You are the Rock of my Salvation, and my High Tower. And I am more than a Conqueror in Jesus Christ Name.

I continued on with my prayer, until the power of God was surging through me. And as I was thanking God I said, now I have dug a well. Because I am not the only one, Satan has tried to kill, in this dry and lonely place.

The next morning after breakfast my grandpa went back into their bedroom. In a moment he returned with a rifle in his hand. He said, come on boy, there are blue jays in my pecan trees. My grandma said, don't call him boy, his name is Donnie. We both stopped and was looking at her smiling, as grandpa said, he is my boy. We both laughed and started out the door again when grandma spoke. Donnie, we both stopped and looked at her, as I said, yes mam. She put her hand to the side of her face, like she was going to whisper. As she said, I don't know what we are going to do with him. I said yes mam. And we all started laughing, as he said,come on boy we have blue jays to kill. I said yes sir, and out the door we went.

He moved his chair so he could see more of the trees. As a blue jay flew into the tree, he shot and killed it. I asked if he would like for me to go and get it? He said, yes please. So I walked out into the yard, picked up the bird and walked back. I was looking at all the pretty colors on the bird when he asked. Did you settle it with God last night? I said yes sir, and I dug a well. He laughed and asked, you did? I said, yes sir.

He said, I am going to ask your dad if you can stay here for a few more nights. There are a lot of spiritual things about you I would like for us to talk about. I said yes sir, there are a lot of things about you, I would like to know to. Then he asked, do you remember being with God before you were born? I said, yes sir I do. I went quite waiting to see where we were going in this conversation. Then he asked, do you remember a dragon? I said, yes sir, I have a dragon, but he belongs to God. He laughed so hard he almost fell out of his chair. He said, I sure hope you can stay, we have a lot to talk about. He was making me laugh to, as I said, yes sir.

Then I asked him, why does Satan want to kill me so bad. He stopped laughing and said, I don't know boy. But you will run into trouble all your life. And God is going to use you, but how I do not know.

Then he said, let's go count the cows, and walk around the farm. I said, yes sir. So he took the rifle back into the house, and I walked towards the barn. I stopped to wait on my grandpa, and the power of God came over me again.

My dad showed up that evening and asked if I had behaved. My grandpa said, oh yes we had a good time. And I would like for you to leave him here for a few days. My dad said, I had better not, school is fixing to start back. And I have to live with his mom, and she will kill me if I don't show back up with him. My grandpa said, I really would like to spend some time with him. And he can go to school over here, and live with me and your mom. My dad said, I have thought about sending him to another school, considering the trouble he has had ever since he started. My grandpa laughed and said, I can see that. My dad said, I will come back in a couple of days and we can talk. My grandpa said, bring him with you. My dad said, I might but you and I need to talk first. My grandpa agreed, I hugged and kissed my grandparents and we left.

On the way home my dad gave me a little history lesson. He said, the room I stayed in was were one of his sisters had died, when she was young. And my grandpa had never gotten over it. I said yes sir. He said, she always kept the window cracked at the top for fresh air. That night it snowed, and grandpa shut the window. She caught pneumonia and died, and grandpa blamed himself for closing the window. I told dad that he came into the room and cracked it at the top when I slept there. He said that was the reason why. I said, yes sir.

Then he asked, did you and grandpa talk? I said, yes sir. We did dad but I think, me changing school's, is not the answer. I will just have to prove myself, and trouble follows me no matter where I go. Then I said, I am entering the eighth grade this year. And I feel before I get out of it, I will hate my own life. He said, you are already a hand full. I said, yes sir, but I don't think you have seen any thing yet. He and I started laughing. Then he said, I can see your mom raised you. Laughing I said, don't blame this one on mom. I will probably just give the world back some of what it's been giving me. And you know I am going to quit school as soon as possible. And I do have an appointment with God. And I don't what to miss that. He said, I was wondering if you had given up on God. I looked at him smiling and said, not in this life time, I am going to Heaven. Then he started smiling again.

As we pulled into the driveway my dad said, I think it would be good for you to get to know your grandpa. He is old now and we don't know how many more years, we will have him with us. I said, yes sir.

I hugged and kissed my mom as we walked through the door. Mom asked if I had a good time? I said, yes mam. She said good, your friend came by and asked where you were. So I told him, he said he would come back tomorrow. I said, thank you. As we sat at the table my dad said the blessing over the food. Mom asked dad if everything was good at his dads? He said it was, and he was going by there tomorrow to talk to him. She said, that would be nice.

That night after reading some scripture from the Bible. I started seeking out God in the Spirit realm. The way I always have done. I was asking God about the gifts of the Spirit. And how they operated. How God being One was Three. And how God has planed out salvation through the life of the earth. It first was through circumcision, salvation was given. Then it came through Jesus Christ crucified on the Cross. And after the Rapture, it will come through not taking the Mark of the Beast.

I was looking at Jesus Christ, and the Holy Spirit. At the many functions they do have, to raise the dead, to heal the sick, to provide for so many people. And I return to water. God always brings me back to water. The substance of all life. God and I talked about my grandpa, and him being a seer. And God has given me the gifts that I have. We talked about the Angle standing at the corner of the field. And grandpa becoming my teacher, on the things he could teach me. Then I asked God about the Dragon, the Spirit took on a very soft and happy feeling, before with drawing from me. And I went to sleep.

I awoke the next morning to my friend standing in the doorway to my room. He was saying, Donnie get up we have to talk. School is starting back Monday and I have a lot to talk to you about. As I threw off the covers and sat up in the bed, he asked, do you always sleep with your clothes on? I said, no it must be something I just started. I put my feet on the floor looking for my boots. I noticed how and were he was standing, deja-vu hit me. He was standing exactly the way he will be, after my appointment with God. I froze looking at him until he asked, what is wrong? I started putting on my boots and say, nothing is wrong. I hugged and kissed my mom goodbye and out the door we went.

As we rode around he said, he was quitting school as soon as he was old enough. I said, so am I. Then I asked, how he was going to support all those children, he was going to have, with no job. A smile came across his face, as he shot me a bird. Then he reached under his seat and pulled out a bottle of liquor. I said, what the hell are we going to do with that. As he turned off the pavement onto a dirt road, he said we are going to drink it, or at least some of it. As we parked on the river bank I said, I love the river. He said, I know you say it every time. As he took a swallow, it made him cough a little, as it took his breath away. Then he passed the bottle to me. I told him I had never drank liquor before. He said, good a couple of snorts should do us. We took a couple of swallows apiece, and then he put the bottle back under the seat.

We walked to the river so we could see it better. I took a deep breath, and could smell the water, the fish, and the flowers that were in bloom. And my skin could feel the moisture from the river. As I looked at him and said, life does not get any better than this. I could hear the little sounds of the river as it was slowly passing by. He looked at me and asked, why life had so much bullshit in it. I started laughing and said, we all have different roads to go down. And different bullshit we have to put up with. Then he asked, what is our purpose for being here. I said, What doors will God open for us to go through. We know God appointed presidents, and formed Government's. He started laughing and said, Donnie do you really believe God appointed our President.

I said, this is God's country, our Constitution was based on the Ten Commandments. We are a light to the world. And my dad said, after

World War One the Jewish people did not have a home. The United States said, according to the Bible, Israel is your home. And we fought for them until they became a Country.

Then he said, you know they put us on a reservation. I laughed and said, they did. We talked for a little while longer and then he took me home.

A few days later my grandpa showed up at school. It was early in the morning before school had taken in. He said, come on boy before we get caught, I said, caught at what? He said, we are playing hooky from school today. I said, grandpa, school has not been going a week yet, and I am already playing hooky. He said, I have cleared it with your dad let's go. So I got into the car and asked, where are we going? He said, fishing, we need to go fishing. I said, yes sir but you are going to get me in so much trouble. He asked, who with your dad, he knows I can still whip his butt. Then he thought for a moment and said, well maybe not, but I used to could. We both started laughing.

As we arrived at the river and got set down, he pointed out a mallard duck. And the fish that was coming to the top of the water. He asked me if I would like to hear a story? I said, yes sir grandpa, I would love to hear a story. He asked me what kind of story I wanted to hear. I said, now grandpa you know there is only one story, and His name is Jesus Christ. And that is what I would love to hear. That made grandpa laugh, and so did I.

From that day forward until grandpa died, he was my teacher. As he taught me,the presence of God became very real to me. And the Holy Spirit would surround us, lifting us higher and higher.

As we sat there quite for a moment then he said, Donnie this world is nothing but trouble. But be of good cheer, God said, He has overcome this world. Grandpa said, trouble in this life is like clouds, sometimes you can see it coming, and are able to prepare for it. And other times you can not, and end up getting wet. Either way Jesus Christ is our shelter. Then he said, this is also the story of Saul and David. Saul ran to the people to try and please them. David ran to God to please Him. So do we serve God and let the world be crazy all around us. Or do we get caught up in the glimmer and start serving the people.

But there is a balance there because we are in the world, but not of the world. Then a soft cool breeze blew and grandpa asked if I could feel it? I said yes sir I can feel that. Then he said, the Holy Spirit is just like that breeze, no one can tell you where it came from, or where it is going. Then he said, my experiences with God are like this. When He gets a hold of you, you don't know where He will take you. Or when you are coming back, but know God is in control. I said yes sir.

As grandpa talked, the power of God ran all over me. He looked at me and said, that power from God that's resting on you. Stay in it as long as you can, that is God building something in you. I said, yes sir I will.

That evening dad came and picked me up. I asked him on the way home, why does God have Satan chained in His throne room? He thought for a moment and said, you will have to ask God that question when you get there. I laughed and said, they both talk to me. But my promises are in God, with my Salvation. When man gets through throwing God out of His own world. God will turn it over to Satan for a season. And then God will destroy the earth one more time. And then God will start it back up again.

My dad said, that is deep thinking for a young man. And from what you were saying the other day. You are going to add a few pages in hell yourself. I laughed and asked, when does a person have to defend himself. And why should he have to resort to violence. My dad said, son the Bible is full of war. And the United States takes the war to them so we can live in peace here. Then he said, you know I am a sniper. I said, yes sir. Then I said, something is going to happen dad and before it is through, I will hate my own life. He said, you need to pray about that. I said, believe me I am looking right at it. And how do you change your future. He said, I do not know.

After a few days I was walking across the yard, looking at the garden. Thinking of things to come, when my cousin came pulling in the driveway. When he saw me he just pulled across the grass to where I was. I asked him what he was doing today. He said he was driving around drinking liquor, thinking about life. Then he asked, if I would come around and get in the truck. I said, yes I could do that. He passed the bottle to me and I took a swallow.

Then he asked, what is life, and why are we here? I said, you are older than I am, and you have been thinking about it, so you tell me. He said, I am trying to have a serious conversation with you. I started laughing and asked, if this was the only bottle of liquor he brought with him. Then he asked, is this all there is to life. I smiled and said, the thing to ask is where are we going after this life. I said, yes this is pretty much it. We grow up get a job, get married, have children, and grandchildren, get old and die. Just like the birds and the bees. He said now that is depressing as hell. I said no not really, the fun part is getting there. That made him smile, and I said, this is the time of life God has picked for us. This is our time on God's calendar to live and have a family and die. He asked, why do you always talk about death? I started laughing and said, I thought you are older than me. Through death I am alive, and in this life I am dead. I am always looking into a Kingdom formed by God. We live in an upside down world, but it runs parallel with the Bible. And God's Kingdom.

My cousin said, you are making my brain hurt, trying to think of what you are saying. Then he said, I heard what happened to you. And they killed the man during a deal that went bad. I said, that is what they say. He asked me, where was God in all of this?

I said, I am alive, and I have a sound mind. It is true I could have blamed God. The blame game started in the Garden of Eden. Job was setting on top of the world. Until satan stepped in and destroyed it all. David was chased by Saul, living in caves. And getting those that came in contact with him killed. Twelve Angels went before God, and one of them was the devil. The Bible is full of rape, murder, lying, cheating, stealing, fornicating, and adultery. But it's also full of Love, Peace, Hope, Joy, Long Suffering, Genteelness, Kindness, and Mercy. Satan would love to stop me in my tracks. Who is it that has chased after God, that has not ran into trials, or tribulations. But the Love of God passes all understanding. And let the Joy of the Lord come and be your strength. And it would have been better for him, if a millstone was hung around his neck, and he was cast into the sea. God is my Peace, and my Concealer. Then I said, sorry about that down load cousin. But should I let Satan rob me of my Salvation. It is not the point Satan knocked me down. It's how long he can keep me down. Before I can rise above it. But God is my Comfort. Know matter what, God will make a way.

Then I went quite gathering my thoughts. My cousin asked, what is it with you and God? I looked at him smiling and asked, what are you asking? He said, I have been hearing some crazy things about you. I said, you have been talking to my friend. He said, what I was told did not come from your friend. But I did ask him about it, and he said it was true. Then I asked, what is it you want to know. He asked me to tell him his future. I said, you want me to prophecy over you. He said yes, as long as it is not anything bad, I don't think I could take that. I said, you and I have been drinking, and I do not think it is a good idea for me to knock on God's door drinking. He asked, if I would try? I said, there is no trying to this, God has already showed me yours. And that got his attention, so I said, I will look again. So I asked him to be quiet for a moment. While he was quite I prayed and God showed me again the same thing as before. So I went through it with him, he would marry, they would have four children, they would buy a farm. They would get a divorce, the children would go with her, child support would be unbearable. He would come to me and we would pray. Two would come and live with him, but they would not stay. Then all of a sudden I said, I am going to get out of the truck now I have things to do. He said, alright Donnie I love you man. And I said, I love you too, and he left.

After watching my cousin leave, I walked into the house. My mom was cooking so I kissed her on the cheek. She said, you have been drinking. I said yes mam, I had a couple of shots with my cousin. She asked, is that the reason he did not come in? I said, yes mam, and we were talking about life. She asked, what we had decided about life? I told her just to live it, and she laughed. Then I said, mom I have something's to talk to God about , I think I will go in my room. She said, supper will be ready soon, I said, yes mam.

I had started reading the Bible again, and the dreams I was having disturbed me. So I asked God, what will men and women do that are left here. After the battle of Armageddon, Your Spirit will be removed. What will they do with out Your great Love, that we all have around us. The Bible says we could not call on you without the prompting of the Holy Ghost. Will they just be empty shells without a since of right or wrong. Living under the power of the Beast, run by Satan.

Then I said, in my experiences I can not have God, without Satan being there. I am not a monk, and I do not live in a monastery. I live in a real world, were I see real people struggling to make right decisions. Now I know there are some bad things coming my way. And only in You,my Lord, my God, and my King am I going to make it. Because I can not protect myself, not against what I see. So I surrender my life to You Father, and in the Name of Jesus Christ I seal my prayer with His Blood. Amen.

So dad started taking me to see grandpa, and we all started farming. As they taught me how life was like for them. It was the best time of my life, and grandpa was still teaching me about God.

One day as I came around the corner of the house. My grandpa said, put the hoe down boy and come here. As I walked over to him setting in a chair, reading the Bible. I could see the power of God on him. As he said, give me your hand. I stuck my hand out and he took it. He mumbled something and then he looked at me and smiled. He said, a Samson anointing is what I have been looking at on you. Nothing in this world will ever hold you, and you will become a wild man. Going here and there searching and looking. But women will be your down fall, but the power of God will never leave you. And when he was through he turned me loose. Then I said, grandpa I don't even know if I like girls yet. He busted out laughing and said, boy, believe me you will. And the way he said it made us both laugh.

CHAPTER 8
July 5, 2021
Autobiography by Donnie Lothridge

This is something that happened to me, and I believe it happened to me right around this time frame. Or it may have been a little before we started farming at grandpas. And it troubled me for years. My dad and I was laying in a field one night. Watching a meteor shower when all of sudden, one of them stopped and stayed there for a minute or two. Then it changed directions, and in a flash it was gone. So I asked him, what was that. He said, that is one of the reasons you and I are out here. God made universes and we are not alone.

A few nights later I was asleep in my bed, when I was taken into a ship. I was lying on a table with a white sheet over me. It was very bright, and when they pull the sheet over my face I would go to sleep. There was a room I would awaken in, it had what looked like bubbling glass jars made in the walls. There was an alien head in each one, but the bodies were not formed yet. We talked with our minds so there was no need to speak. When I was in this room there was a band around my head. And it operated other things hooked to my body. When they were through with me in this room, and they were putting the sheet over my head, to put me to sleep. That band on my head would scramble my thought pattern, of what just happened.

There was another room I awoke in, and it had a lot of tables in it like the one I was laying on.

I can remember being moved from one ship to another, and also coming very close to God's planet.

How long they kept me I can not say, but I felt if they had not brought me back, I would have died.

Years later I was working on a dairy. It was my day off, so I was fishing on one of their ponds. When all of a sudden I could feel them again. So I said, beam me up Scottie there is no intelligent life forms down here. The sun acted like it was hidden behind some clouds. But the temperature became hotter instead of cooler, so I looked up to see. And there was a big triangle shaped ship hovering over the pond. There was no sound of it, or wind from it, as it set perfectly still in the air. A few feet above the tree tops. The only thing I could fill was the heat from it. I thought I was being burned from heat, so I took a step backwards. And when I did the ship slowly turned, hovering away from the pond. And in a flash it was gone.

Then I had thoughts of the last time I had an encounter with them. And it made my knees weak.

Now I have failed the eight grade, and I have watched as my grandpa's walking has gotten worse. And I know he is planning on going into the hospital for an operation. I also know he will never recover. It is in early spring and school has just let out. God and I are having a little talk about life, while I am preparing the garden. I said, well God my life is in the shit'er, and I do not know where I am going in life. But I trust in You. Then a flash of my alien encounter ran through my mind. And that really aggravated me. As I am fussing I said, I don't even know why I am talking to You. Sometimes You are so Powerful and Present, and other times I know you are there but I can not reach You. Then I got distracted plowing the garden, and at the end of plowing I asked for forgiveness.

We went to grandpa's and prepared the field's there. Before long it was Good Friday, and we planted the field's. Then I started hoeing the garden at our house, around the tomatoes we had planted. I started talking to God again. And then I started fussing, like I was finishing the conversation we started weeks ago. I had hoed about two rows in this state of mind, and I was coming to the end of the second row. When I asked, so were do You go God, when I can not reach You? Then I said, and I will tell You another thing, I will not serve a God that will not talk to me. At that moment I definitely had God's attention, as I was hit with His Mighty Power. And I flew through the air about ten feet, landing in the yard. I lay there unable to move as God's sweet Holy Spirit, like waves flowed through me, over and over.

As I got up I staggered backwards into the yard, almost falling down again. I was catching myself as I was looking for the hoe. Saying thank You, Father God, Jesus Christ, and the Holy Ghost. I found the hoe, still drunk in the Spirit I leaned against it. I screamed out Hallelujah, as I stood there for a minute. With the power of God still running through me. I walked back up to the house, and when I came through the back door my mom started laughing. Asking, what has happened to you? I could see the power of God was resting on her to. I said, mom I just had an experience with God. As I sat down on the couch. She said, I would say you did Donnie. As she started laughing, I could tell the Spirit was all over her to. We set there for quite some time enjoying the Power of God. That was there with us. (What If?)

As we started farming at grandpa's it was fishing, checking fish baskets, running trout lines, checking set hooks, and farming. So my schedule for the summer was packed. And grandpa and us had the time of our life. But grandpa also knew his time was short. So he poured all of himself he could into me, of his walk with God.

The greatest lesson he ever gave me was, get out of the boat. Looking always at your options, were will God open the door. Do not get trapped looking at things one way. And always look for your next move. With Satan it is always a dead end. With God it is building blocks, preparing you for the next move. I would always say yes sir, when he was through talking to me. Even at my age, I knew he was speaking into my life. He was seeing things I could not yet see. And I was seeing things I did not like, and a lot of times I did not understand at all.

Now my dad's thought on it all of this was, I am getting you in shape. Because basically people are good, but because of what you have already been through. It's time to get mean, and start fighting back. And from hauling hay, and living life farming. He had me in pretty good shape. He also was preparing me for the military, as how to become one with nature. Will she expose you, or will she hide you. Will you learn how to survive in her, or will she kill you. Everything has a Spirit, and nature will kill you, if you do not respect her.

Now this would be the last fishing trip, my grandpa and I would ever take. He knew it, and I guess he told me in his own way. We had been fishing and laughing all morning. Caught up in the spirit, of being on the water, and enjoying life. We were getting ready to move to another spot to fish. When grandpa said, let's go up the lake there is a cove up there I have not fished in years.

So I cracked the boat up, and up the lake we went. Watching the little fish jumping beside the boat, and the beautiful water cranes fishing to.

As we were getting close to the spot grandpa wanted to fish. He said, slow the boat down boy, right around that point in front of us, is were I want to fish. I said yes sir, so I slowed the boat down. He said, you are still going to fast, slow the boat down some more. I said yes sir, so now we are moving very slow. And I asked him, grandpa what are we looking for? He said, I am looking for Jesus Christ to come walking to me on the water. I said grandpa, He has already done that a few times. Grandpa laughed and said, get out of the boat boy. If you never get out of the boat, you will never learn how to walk on the water. I said grandpa, I live out of the boat most of the time. Grandpa laughed and said, I see.

My cousin started asking questions, trying to find out why grandpa and I, spent so much time together. But grandpa and I had a relationship that was solid, and it was all about God. Grandpa was my teacher and grandpa knew it.

One of the things he taught me was always build a bridge. Know matter where life takes you, know matter were you find yourself, build a bridge. We are called by God, to build that bridge, to climb that mountain, to be with God, Father, Son, and Holy Ghost. Build that closeness to God, because time's will not always be this good. God has laid out His plan and we all are a very important part of it. My grandpa said, I have lived through the depression and raised a family. That was my time. Your dad is living out his time, and raising a family. And you have just started your time, and your adventures with God. And you know the two forces that are here. And you know right now God is going to win, were you are concerned. I said, yes sir.

Then he said, you and I both know Satan wants to destroy you. I said, yes sir. Then he said, but God has already won, what God has done in the past, He will do in the future. Then he started laughing and said, boy you would not believe the man I was, and what I am today. God will never give up on any of us, because His love endures forever. I said, yes sir.

A few days later my grandpa went into the hospital. In two or three days my mom told me that grandpa was coming home tomorrow. And that everything was going to be fine. I said, no mam it is not going to be fine, grandpa will die tomorrow. Upset she said I should not speak such things. I said, mom he and I both know, that he is going home to be with God. She put her head down and walked off.

The next day one of my uncle's stopped by on the way to the hospital. He was supposed to pick me up to go with him, but my mom would not let me go, because of what I had told her. My uncle said, he was there waiting for his release, when a blood clot broke loose, went to his heart and killed him. I had came into the house from working in the garden. When the phone rang and it was my uncle with the news. After hanging up the phone my mom told me my grandpa had died. Then she busted out crying and told me to go to my room. On the way down the hall I looked back at her and said,it will be O.K.

In my room I sat on the bed, I could hear mom on the phone with dad. I turned to the Spirit realm and started talking to God about grandpa. I stood up and started walking the floor in my room. I asked, God who would be my teacher now. When I asked that, I was knocked to the floor by the power of God. Lying with my face to the floor God dressed me. I had a crown on my head, it was not one that stood up. It was a band of gold, about two or three inches wide, with jewels in it. I was wearing clothes, and I had a rode, that fit across my shoulders, and went down my back to the bend of my knees. Around my waist was a belt. On my chest was a breast plate, and in front of me was my helmet, sword, and shield. Then God spoke to me and said, I am your teacher now, and the world is my classroom. Then Satan spoke and asked, Heaven or Earth, Heaven or Earth, were would you like your reward. I said, Heaven of course. Then they were gone. I said, now you remember I have to live down here. Then the vision of what God was showing me went away.

We went to my grandparents house, my cousin and I was standing outside mourning my grandpa's death. After us crying for a while he asked, why were you spending so much time with grandpa? I said, The truth is he was teaching me the way he walked in the Spirit. He said, and all the fun you and he had. I smiled and said, they were lessons in life, and in the Spirit realm. He said, I went fishing with him, but he never did any of that with me. I said, it is because you are a physical person and want things in life, you can see and touch. And I am drawn into the Spiritual realm, God and the hereafter. It does not mean, that I don't want things in life. I do they are just not my mane concern. And I am not focused like you are. He said, so that makes me smarter than you. We started laughing and I said, no but you will hate me in the end. We both stopped laughing and started thinking about grandpa again.

And then at the funeral, after everyone almost had left. I told my cousin to come with me, because I could see we all were going to have problems with this. I led him to the grave and got a hand full of dirt. I said, now you get you a hand full of dirt to, and he did, and he said, now what. I said, now say goodbye to grandpa, and when you can feel his peace and love, turn loose of the dirt and say goodbye. And so we both did. Then he asked, is this supposed to help? I said, You know grandpa is at peace, and we felt his love. And we said, goodbye for now, we will be with him again on the other side. And he lives in all of us, so yes it is supposed to help. My cousin said, well Donnie it sure as hell don't feel like it right now. That made us both stop crying and start laughing. Then he said, I do feel better, but if I want to talk about grandpa, I am coming to your house. I said, yes sir any time. (What If?)

CHAPTER 10

July 8, 2021

Autobiography by Donnie Lothridge

A few days after grandpa had passed away, I am working in the garden. God and I are talking about me quitting school. And the Storms in my Spirit I am looking at. The bitterness of my grandpa being gone. How life is changing, and how to change the path I am on. My appointment with God flashes through my mind, of when I said it to my friend in the beginning. Then all the visions God had shown me, the good and the bad. The fear of what was ahead of me. I stopped hoeing for a moment to take a break. I said, Lord God, if I cannot control what will happen, then I turn it all over to you. And I pray that You take control of every situation that I find myself in. In Jesus Christ Name I pray, Amen.

As I started working again, I see a car pulling into the driveway. It was a cousin. I thought now there comes trouble, as a smile came across my face. As he gets out of the car, and walk towards me. My cousin asked, do you feel like taking a break. I said, I do, and I am very glad to see you.

He asked, is there a place we can set down in the shade. I said, there is behind the pole barn the grass is soft there. As we sat down he gave his condolences about my grandpa. I said, yes we are going to miss him, but he was ready to go home, and be with the Lord.

My cousin said, Donnie there is something I would like to talk to you about, to see what you think about it. I asked, you are not fixing to throw me to the wolves are you? He started laughing and said, no it's nothing like that. Then he pulled out a plastic bag from his pocket, and asked, if I knew what it was. As he handed it to me and asked me to smell it. And I did and said, it smells very good what is it. He said it's called, Marijuana and you smoke it, and it gets you high. He pulled out some rolling papers, and started rolling a joint. As I asked, and how much trouble can we get into for this.

He said, we can be arrested for it, but the money will go to support the war. He lit it and passed it to me, I took a drag off of it. And said, it tastes very good, and passed it on. Saying so the government is putting it out, and taking it up. He said, yes as he took a hit off of it and passed it back to me. I said, as I took a hit and passed it back, now that sounds like the greatest mind fuck I have heard yet. We started laughing as he said, our people helped the government during the Indian wars. And then they put us on the reservation with the rest of them. Then we really started laughing.

Then he asked me if I could grow it? I said, if it has seeds I can grow it.

Then I asked, were did it come from, and he said, it came from another country. And he started educating me on Marijuana. I listened to all he had to say. And he asked me to think about growing it. He gave me some of it to smoke later, and I noticed there were seeds in with it. As he started to leave he said, he would be back in a few days. I told him thank you for the education, and it sounded like he had put a lot of time in learning about it. He smiled and said, I have.

In a few days my cousin showed back up. I was working in the garden again, and he asked, if I was ready for a break? I said yes, and I was very glad to see him again. He asked if I was alright with my grandpa's death? And I said, it's hard but yes I am doing fine. Then I said, let's set over here were we did last time, it's in the shade and the grass is soft. I asked how he was doing, and he said, it was all good.

As we sat down he pulled out another bag of Marijuana, and we started talking about it again. I asked him how serious he was about this adventure he wanted to go on. He said, he was not sure yet, because he had not looked at all the ins and outs of it. I told him to hold up on rolling a joint, I still had what he had left. As I went into the house to retrieve the bag of weed, I noticed my corn cob pipe and picked it up to. As I returned to my cousin he started laughing and said, you want to smoke it through this thing? I said, I don't know it was just an idea. He said, let's see this thing, as he took it from me. He took it apart and threw the filter across the yard. He said, we don't need this, and we don't need to smoke it all the way to the bottom.

I started laughing and he asked, what is it? I said, you never cease to amazing me. He laughed and asked, what are friends for? We smoked out of the pipe and passed it back and forth. He noticed the bag he had given me was not touched. I told him I had smoked one out of it, and I like the taste, and the high it gave me. But I had a lot of questions concerning what he was asking about.

He said, funny you should say something like that, I have been talking to a man about you. And he would like to meet you. I said, now is when you throw me to the wolves. He said, no if you do not want to meet him, I will drop the hole thing. I said, I did not say that I would not meet with him, I have some questions he might be able to answer. He said, good because I have already arranged it. I will pick you up tomorrow after lunch.

The next day he shows up about one-thirty. I was ready and had already asked mom if I could go. So I was clear on everything, I just hugged and kissed my mom goodbye, and she said, be careful as I went out the door. As I walked down the steps, I said, I would be careful and got in the car. On the way over to were we were going we smoked a joint. My cousin was acting very nervous, so I asked him what was up. And if he knew what he was getting me into? He did one of those silly little laughs he does and said, I have know idea? So I asked him, what if you get me killed. He started laughing and said, well hell we better smoke another joint. As we got close to the house, car's were back up waiting there turn. I asked, what the hell is this? He almost wrecked the car laughing. Then I said, well if I don't see you no more in this life, I will definitely be waiting on you in the next one. We started laughing as he said, we have to stop this laughing we are almost to the house. Then he said, the man in the driveway, will open your door, when he does do what he says. I said, yes sir. Laughing time was definitely over with.

As we pulled into the circle drive my cousin said, I will drive around for about an hour, then I will come back and pick you up. I said, thank you. As we approached the man in the driveway. He opened my car door and I stepped out. He said, hello Donnie you look just like your dad. I said, thank you sir. My cousin spoke up and said, I will be back after while to pick you up. The man in the driveway said, you can come back and check. But I do not think he will be riding back with you. My cousin and I both said, yes sir at the same time. Traffic was starting to back up so the man in the driveway said, you can leave now we have Donnie. I watched as he pulled around the circle drive and left. I could tell from the expression on my cousin's face, he was thinking, this is not the smartest thing he had ever done.

Then the man in the driveway spoke up and said, go own into the house they are waiting for you. I said yes sir. As he said, watch out for those dogs, I would hate for you to lose an arm or a leg. I said yes sir, again, as I walked up the steps. And he was not telling a story, I walked between two Doberman Pincher, teeth and snapping jaws was all I could see.

As I knocked on the screen door frame, I could see a big man sitting in a recliner chair, smiling at me. He says, who in the hell is that knocking on my door, no one knocks on my door, come on in. I said yes sir thank you. As I step inside the door I am looking at a man with a full beard. And all of a sudden, a woman comes through the house, and grabbed me by the arm. She says, so this is Donnie Carroll Lothridge, you look just like your dad, and how is your mom. I have not seen them in years. And the last time I seen you, you were in diapers. I said, yes mam. Then she said, I am very sorry about the loss of your grandpa, I will miss him. I said, yes mam me to, and thank you. She said, we would have came to the funeral but we are unable to leave this place. I said, yes mam.

Then she said again, I cannot believe how much you look like your dad. I said, thank you mam. Then the man setting in the chair clearing his throat and said, woman if you don't turn him loose, and set down where he and I can talk. Then she turned me loose looking at him, and threw her hair back walking past him. She asked, how rude can you be? And took a seat on a couch.

As I am standing there the man starts mumbling. The man comes and knocked on my door, and no body knocks on my door. Then he says, yes mam to my wife, and yes sir to me, what the hell is this world coming to. Well, you are here now so let's talk. You can have a seat on the couch, and then you can explain to me, what the hell you are doing here. His wife spoke up and said, you invited him here. He said, I know that, I wanted to hear what he was going to say.

I said, we have an appointment to see each other today. He said, very good I like that answer. Let's move to the table so we can talk, as we all stood up, l noticed the pistol he had lying in his lap. He said, you set at that end of the table, so I sat with my back to the window. Then he told his wife, you set here, that put her back to the sink, and the kitchen windows. Then he sat at the other end of the table, that put his back against the refrigerator. He put the pistol on the table and it was pointed in my direction. His wife asked me if I would like a glass of water? I said, no thank you. She got her a glass of water, and started rolling a joint. He said, you are reading my mind. Then she lit it and we passed it around.

That is when he asked me, what are you looking for? Then he leaned back in his chair, opened the refrigerator and took out two beers. Opening one he slid it to me. His wife said, he is not thirsty, I asked him. He said, I didn't ask him, but if we are going to talk about weed, he is going to drink a beer with me. I said, we can do that, now what are you looking for? A smile came across his face, as he said, they tell me you would like to learn how to grow weed. I said, it has seeds don't it. Before I could finish what I was trying to say, I was looking down the barrel of his pistol. And looking at the hallow points, he had in the revolver.

He asked, what kind of smart ass are you? How about I just go ahead and blow a fucking hole in you, I can drive a car threw.

I started laughing and said, because if you do that I am going to bleed all over her kitchen floor. Glancing at her I could see her mouth had fell open in everything she was seeing and hearing. Then I said, and she will have to clean it up, and she will be so mad at you. You will not get none of her for a month.

He started laughing and let the hammer down on the revolver, lying the pistol on the table. She still looks like a frozen cat, with her mouth open. He and I are now laughing at her, then she jumped up saying you lied to me. Y'all do know each other and started slapping him. He was laughing so hard, and trying to catch her arms saying I did not lie, I have never meet him before today. When he finally got her pulled into his lap and calmed down. She said, y'all played a joke on me, y'all do know each other. He said, then ask Donnie if we have ever met before today. He and I are still laughing as I say, no mam, I have never seen him before today. We all started laughing and smoked another joint.

Then I asked, can I finish what I was trying to say before you pulled the pistol on me? He said, you can but you better be careful the way you word things. That made us laugh again.

Then the man from the driveway came in and said, his friend is back to pick him up, what shall I tell him? He said, tell him we will take him home. So he went and told him and he left. Then I picked up our conversation again in my interest in growing. He told me he would talk to the man he worked for, and let me know. I said, thank you. Then he said, drop the sir, and the mam, it makes us and everyone else something we are not. I know from your dad, it is respect, we might be working for our Government, but we are not military. And they will put our asses in prison like everyone else. I said, I can not get my mind to settle that, it's to much of a mind fuck for me. He smiled and said, it's all fucked up Donnie, the war and everything. I smiled and said, there are a lot of brave men that are well trained, given there lives, and for what. He smiled and said, let's smoke another joint. I said, yes let's burn another one.

As we finished the joint, his wife and I were tracing back how our families crossed. When he spoke up and said, Donnie I have been thinking about you settling this in your mind. I have heard you are a very spiritual person, and I am just going to tell you the truth. This is a drug house, and you know that. But we are in public service, a demand, and a supply. Here we only do one thing, and that is meet the demand with cash only. We do not deal with any stolen property, or anything that is against the law. Other than what we do. If you see me do it, it is not the way this house is run. I am getting it for myself, and I am backing it up with my cash. I said, yes sir, and he corrected me on the sir.

As the sun was setting. We rolled another joint and they asked me if I would like to spend the night. They said everything slows down around eleven, except for them bagging weed for the next day. I said, I would like to but I really needed to get home. I have some work to finish in the garden in the morning. They said, they could square it with my dad if I changed my mind. I said, thank y'all but I am needed back home.

The mans wife spoke up and said, I would like to take him home if I could. I would like to see Donnies mom again. He said, that it would be fine, but for her not to stay long, they had work to do. She hugged and kissed her husband goodbye. And then I said goodbye to her husband. He said, I will see you again in a few days, with your answer. I said,thank you, and out the door she and I went. I went out the door first and held it open for her to come through. I was not thinking about the Doberman Pincher at the door. When I heard the dog growl I took a half step forward, and pulled in my ass. As the dog's slobber wet the seat of my pants, I could feel the dogs breath. She said to her husband who was laughing, I told you them dog's were to close to this door. Laughing he said, they are supposed to be. The man in the driveway was laughing to as he said, that was almost your ass. I said, you are not kidding about that, as I was wiping dog slobber off the seat of my pants.

As she and I walked to her car she asked, what I thought about her husband. As we got into the car I said I like him. As we rode down the road she said, he really likes you. I have not seen him act like that towards anyone ever. I asked her laughing was that before he tried to shoot me or afterwards. She laughed and said, y'all pulled a joke on me, y'all do know each other. I said, no mam I have never seen your husband before today. She said, y'all scared the shit out of me. I said, yes mam and believe me, I was feeling your pain looking down the barrel of that pistol. She laughed and said, he really does like you. You kept him laughing about all day. I said, yes mam but he was very serious about what he had to say. She said I know, he was not bull shitting you. He told you just the way it is, like you did him. I said, yes mam. She said, I like you being so polite, but he is right to say don't do it around our house. Especially around people that are not important, then she said, you know what I mean, it shows weakness not caricature. I said, yes mam.

As we pulled into the driveway she said, you are different from anyone I have ever met. The aura that you put off is very strong. And from the reaction my husband had towards you he felt it to. I said he was right, I am very spiritual, but I am battling in the spirit realm. And the things I am looking at in the future scare the hell out of me. She smiled as she put the car into park. And asked if she could see my mom. I said, of course come on in the house.

As we entered the house I hugged and kissed my mom. And she was very glad to see my mom. Mom fixed them a cup of coffee, and they sat down to talk. She thanked mom for allowing me to come over. Mom said, she did not know were I had went. So she asked if I could come back over later, and mom said yes. Then they talked about my dad, and how much he and I looked alike. Then the mans wife said she had to leave, and apologized for not being able to talk longer. As I walked her back out to her car she said, I will see you later this week Donnie. And I do want to talk to you about spiritual things. I said, yes mam, and she left.

Back in the house my mom said, she was so glad she was able to see the mans wife again. And told me a little bit more about her, and her family. Then my mom asked me if that was Marijuana she smelled on me. I said, yes mam it is, do you like the way it smells I asked? She smiled and said, I have smelled it before. Then she said, she smelled like it to. I said, yes mam, her husband smoked some with us. She smiled and said, I have heard some things about them and what they do. I said, yes mam. She said, I am not going to say weather it is right or wrong, all I can say is be careful and mind your manners. I said, yes mam, then she said, Donnie putting it in a sock, in your sock drawer, is not hiding it. I asked hiding what? She said your stash of Marijuana. I laughed and asked, is that what I did? She said, you know I do the laundry. And I am always going through your room. I said, yes mam, I guess you found my true detective magazines to? She said, I have and I have read a couple of them. And I do not approve of them, they are about violence, torture, and murder. I said, yes mam but they do help my reading skills. See smiled and said, I bet they do. After that I went to bed.

I thought about God, and were my life was going. I also thought about my appointment with death. Then I thought about looking down the barrel of the pistol, and that made me laugh. I also tried to see what being in God's Throne Room would be like. But the vision was kept from me. The brightness of my Father was all I could see. So I went to sleep asking God to hold me, and guide my path. (What If?)

The next day my cousin showed up, and we talked about our adventure. I told him everything was on hold, until we were cleared on being taught how to grow it. We were smoking a joint in my room until my mom smelled it. And then she said, alright boys, or should I say young men, no Marijuana smoking in the house. Donnie you know your dad will have a fit, if he comes home and smelled it. So y'all take that stuff outside to smoke it. We said, yes mam as we went out on the porch with it. He stayed for a few hours and left.

As I walked to the garden across the yard, I thought about the visions, God had shown me. A lot of them were about people trying to take my life. I ask God, is this the world at this time in space. And I knew no matter what, God's love is there for everyone. It's a question of what road we are traveling on. Can I see God at work, can I feel His presence, can I be used for God's purpose here on earth.

And then I would see the darkness, that I knew desired to have me. I felt if that ever happened to me, I would not be myself anymore. I asked God, why knowing all of this, do I forget and darkness over takes me. Knowing the life in the visions are true, is this what You have for me God? I already live a life of deja vu, knowing I have already lived the life I am in. But in the darkness there is Light, and in the Light there is darkness. And every road in life I go down there is a lesson. And I am in need of a Savior, because I can not save myself. And You have already paid that price for me, and have given a country away for me. And as for me and my household, we shall serve the Lord. And not a creation of Yours. Then I said, thank You Lord. Thank You.

So the rest of that day, I spent playing a game with the Lord. I would first ask how many blades of grass are in this yard? And then I would say, the Lord knows. Then I would ask, how many four leaf cloves are there, in this clover patch? Then I would say, the Lord knows. How many clouds are in the sky? The Lord knows. How many feathers are on that bird? The Lord knows. How many gallons of water run down this creek every day? The Lord knows. How many hairs are on my head? The Lord knows. I did that until the sun went down.

Because even though I did not think about it that often. I knew to fall into the presence of the Lord, was going to be a horrible experience. And it was one of those things I hoped to be alone when it happened. I did not want my brother or sister with me. If you knew you would be killed tomorrow how would you live today. Or knowing you had an appointment with God, and it was not very far away. Now how was God going to arrange our appointment. (What If?)

CHAPTER 11

Autobiography by Donnie Lothridge

Now in a few days my cousin showed up again . And he told me my other mom and dad wanted to see me. So we asked, my real mom if I could go and she said yes. So I hugged and kissed her and out the door we went. On the way over there he pulled a joint out from on top of his ear. Fired it up and passed it to me, then we pulled over on a back road. He said, you and I have been through a lot together. And I want you to tell me the truth. What do you think about them after your visit. I said, I love them they are very nice. He asked, then you are alright with everything? I said, I am. Then he said, don't let nothing happen to you over there. I said, I don't think anything will. He said, I feel responsible for getting you into this. I said, that is another thing I have thought about. I do not want to get into something I can't get out of.

He turned the car around and we continued with our trip. On the way over there I said, I liked it when you said, my other mom and dad. He said, I noticed it kinda stuck with you when I said it. I said, it did in a way. He said, you are way to gullible for what I have gotten you into, is what I think. I asked him how else am I going to learn. Unless I can trust who is teaching me. Then I said something that shocked us both. I said, besides I have an appointment with God. He said, I don't want to talk about that. I said, it does not matter I can't change it, and you can't change it. So what ever happens is going to happen. He said, that is one hell of a way to look at death. I said, I will only be gone for a little while, and then I will be back. As we pulled in behind the cars waiting in line, to get to the house. He said, thank God we are almost here. I said, I don't know of any other way to be with my Father.

He asked, why do you talk about that for? Donnie sometimes I do not understand you. Oh they said, they were taking you home. I said, thank you, but I figured that much.

As the man in the driveway opened my car door, he said, hello Donnie. I said hello, he said, they are waiting on you, just go on in. And watch them dogs, as he started laughing. My cousin left and as I got close to the door I noticed the dogs chain's had been shortened. That made me laugh as I reached for the door-handle and stopped. I had never just walked into someone else house before, so I knocked. The man was setting in the recliner looking at me again. He said, oh my God it's mr. polite again knocking on my door. Come on in mr. polite. As I stepped through the door he was laughing. And his wife said, you leave him alone I like it. I said, mom, dad is acting a little mean towards me today don't you think. We all started laughing, and from that day forward I always called them mom and dad.

They asked if I needed anyting to drink? I said, I am good. Then I asked if I could set down, and they said, sure have a seat. He said, I do not have much time today I have to be somewhere else. And I have not gotten in touch with the man I work for. But I do want to talk to you about growing. When my wife was over at your house she noticed your mom's plants. I said, yes sir my mom likes to grow African Violets. He said, it is late in the summer so there is know way to do an outside grow. So I want you to experiment inside with plants. With no natural sun light. And only natural fertilizer. She spoke up and asked if he knew what time it was? Then he said, I have to run but maybe I can make it back before you have to take Donnie home. Unless he would like to spend the night. Then he stood up with the pistol in his hand, that was lying in his lap. Hugged and kissed his wife and told her, he would be back latter. I had stood up when he stood up. Then he said, finish explaining to him the experiments to try. As he approached me he stopped, hugged and kissed me on the side of the head. Then he said, I will see you later son. I said, thanks dad be careful, and out the door he went.

As I turned and looked at his wife standing in unbelief, I smiled. She asked, did he just do what I think he did? I said, he did and he called me son to. She busted out laughing and asked, what is this world coming to? Then she said, well I guess it's final now. We have adopted you. Smiling I looked at her and asked, how lucky can one man be? To have three sets of parents in one lifetime. She looked at me puzzled and asked, three? I said, yes mam God the Father, Son, and Holy Spirit, is my Father. She looked at me as if she was looking through me and asked, that is the Aura that surrounds you isn't it? I said, yes mam. She asked, my, my what are you doing here. I said, you and dad are going to teach me how to grow weed. She said, that we are, but you don't belong here. I asked, were do I belong? She said, I do not know.

Then she walked over to the table and said, this is the way we do it. As she took out a set of scales, the trash bag of weed, and a box of sandwich bags. Then she laid a sandwich bag on the scales. Saying see what it weighs, clearing the scales to zero, she said now we can start weighing out ounces. I said, yes mam. She said, I want you to watch what I am doing, and at the same time, I am going to teach you how to perform, some basic experiments on starting and growing weed. I said, yes mam. She said, we are not looking for you to be great at it now. Because with each failure there is a lesson in what did I do wrong.

As I watched her bag weed, she explained the three different ways she wanted me to sprout the seeds. And for me to pick the best one for me. She said, for the light, my husband said, no natural sun light. That means in a inclosed area like a closet, or a small area. Now in this experiment you have to produce light, air flow, and control the smell of what you have planted. Not to mention water, fertilizer, and how to control pest naturally. Now my husband does not have you cleared with who he works for. So he may tell you this part of it is over. I said, yes mam, then she gave me a bag with a lot of seeds in the bottom of it. Smiling she said, this should get you started. I looked at the sack she gave me and smiled. Then she took a hand full of seeds and laid them on the table. She looked at me and asked me to pick out the female seeds. The male plants are of no value in growing weed. Unless you are looking for seeds, the male plants will rein your entire crop. I asked her to explain it to me in depth, and she did. She said, this is like no plant you have ever grown before. So we want you to have fun in trying to grow it. There is a life time of adventure right here. I said, from what I have learned just listening to you, this is going to be very challenging. She laughed and said I am glad.

Then we looked at the time and it had flown by. She said,I have to get you home. The potting soil your mom uses is not except-able, because the fertilizer is already in it. But it will do for our experiments. I said, yes mam as we left there house and got into her car. I thanked her for allowing me to pick her brain. She said, I have done nothing, until you do it and feel the excitement, of getting this plants through each stage of their lives. That will make me happy. I said, yes mam, mom, and she laughed. As she reached into her pocket book that was between our seats and pulled out a joint. She handed it to me and said, lite it, I want us to smoke this before I get you home. I said, yes mam and lit it, I took a hit off of it and passed it to her. She asked me again why are you here. You know you belong in a church. I said, I have tried a church. She said, I have heard, but the Aura that you give off, do you feel it as strong as I do? I said, probably not, God has knocked me out with it before. She said, I have felt it on your grandpa like this. I said, yes mam probably more off of him than me. She asked, how did you get this? I said, hours of searching, hungry for more than this life could ever give me. Knowing I am only in this life for a little while. And knowing what ever chooses I make here determine where I spend eternity at. If I know I came from Heaven, why would I not want to go back to Heaven, and be with God. She said, Donnie I feel weird smoking weed, and talking to you about God. I asked, are you going to tell me God did not put these things here for our enjoyment. And as long as it is not a problem with us we can enjoy them. But when we lean on the creation, instead of the creator, then it becomes a problem. It becomes our God. As we pulled into my driveway she said, I don't know what I am going to do with you son. We both started laughing and I said, love me like Jesus does mom. Then she handed me the bag of weed I had left on the table. She said, don't forget this. As I got out of the car I said, thank you mom I love you. She said, thank you, and I love you too. Then she turned the car around and left.

As I walked into the house my mom was up. She said, it is a little late for you to be coming in. I said, yes mam, as I hugged and kissed her. I said, I was with the woman you like, her husband had to leave, and I tried to stay until he came back. But it did not work out that way. She said, I know who you were with, and you smell like weed again. I said, yes mam. Mom do you have any extra potting soil that I can have.

She started to smile and said, Donnie Carroll, you are not growing Marijuana in this house. I said, mom it's not growing it, I want to experiment with it. And she said, no Donnie it is against the law. I said,but mom I need to do this. She said, not in this house and that is the end of this discussion. I said, yes mam we can talk more about it tomorrow. Then I kissed her goodnight, telling her I loved her and went to bed.

The next morning I awoke to find myself praying, or talking to God. Thanking Him for another beautiful day, and asking for His help.

I walked in the kitchen and fixed a cup of coffee. My mom was setting on the couch reading the Bible. I came back to the couch were she was, gave her a kiss and sat down. She closed the Bible and said, you are growing up to fast. I kinda laughed, and said, yes mam, I can't tell weather I am living in a dream or a night mare. She laughed and said, you are changing. I said, for the worst I fear. I asked, why are we surrounded by death and violence.

She said, with people and the war going on, it is the time we are living in. People act out on what they are feeling, and that does not make it right. But that is in the world. In here we have peace and love. But bad things happen, and we can not change that. We have to keep on living, and except it now matter what it was. And hope, and pray we were not the cause of it, or caught up in it. Inside the walls of this house is our peace, this is were the Love of God is. It is were your dad and I have built our garden of eden. To raise our family, in peace and love. I think we have done pretty good so far, and one day you will try to do the same. I said, thank you mom. She said, you are welcome, now there is a bag of potting soil under the car port. I am not going to tell you I agree with what you are doing. And if your dad catches you, he will whip your butt and I am going to laugh. Because I do not know anything about it. Smiling I said, thank you mom, I love you. She said, I love you too.

My mom had me thinking about all the bad things I was seeing in my visions, and I was asking God would all this happen before our appointment?

That's when my friend pulled into the driveway. As we greeted each other he asked, if I could go for a ride with him? He wanted to talk to me about everything going on. I laughed and said, of course, then I said, raise a child in the way they should go, and when they are old, they will not depart for it. He asked, are you talking to me? I said, I was talking, but not to you. It's more like a confirmation, of something I was asking God, before you should up. He said, ask your mom and let's go. So I did and we left.

As we parked near the river he rolled a joint, and I took a swallow of liquor. He said, you know after school takes in I am quitting this year. I said, I figured that much. He said, I have had all the bull shit I can take. I said, I am right behind you on quitting school. As we smoked the joint, and took a couple of swallows of liquor. He said, tell me the truth, are you alright with everything? I thought everything, then I asked, are we talking about God, or life? He said, I thought they were the same, God is life. I said, yes God is life, but who will we serve with our life. Will it be this world or God. He said, you know you are around some very dangerous people. I said, I seem to run into that know matter who I am with. Hell you can get drug behind a school bus just going to school, or raped. He busted out laughing as he rolled up another joint, he said, I was laughing about the school bus. I said, I know. Then I said, if I could quit school today I would.

He asked, what is happening to us? I said, I think we are growing up. We laughed and talked for a little while and he took me back home. I started my experiments growing weed. And kept going over to my other mom and dad's house. I was cleared to grow weed, and also on learning how to run the house. I almost burned our house down using a spot light in the closet. Then I switched over to fluorescent lights. I became very mean, and cussing every other word. And I fought at school, I hated myself and everyone else. And I had become what I hated the most, a bully. But even then sometimes a light would go off, so I could take a good look at what I really was.

My daughter asked me about this time in my life. It was before I had my appointment with God. She asked, if I had been turned over to Satan for a season. All I can say is it lasted for three years, and ended with my appointment with God. I learned a lot of lessons during this time. And when I was approached later in life with these problems by Satan. My answer is always the same, that part of me is dead. But I learned the power of witchcraft, sorcery, voodoo, and also had roots put on me. To be pulled and driven by demonic spirits controlled by other people. People Channeling opening doors in the spirit realm into other peoples lives. Just like the curse that was put on our people that fought in the Vietnam War.

My friend quit school when he became of legal age to do so. And I did the same. One day after that my cousin came by and said, your other mom and dad would like to see you. So I asked my mom, and she said, yes I could go. He said, I guess I will drop you off the way I always do. I said, that will probably work. As we were setting in the line he asked, have you noticed how long this line is getting now? I said, I have, as we rolled a joint and smoked it. He said, have you noticed how mean you have become. I said, life has made me this way. And you have changed to, for the worst I might add. We both laughed as he asked, do you know what you are doing. I said, not really but maybe we can get an answer on growing weed. He said, I bet he has done forgotten us. I said, he has not forgotten. As we pulled up the man in the driveway opened my door and said, go on in they are waiting for you. I said thank you, and he said, mr polite. My cousin left, and I went into the house.

As I hugged my new mom and dad they said, set down Donnie we would like to talk to you. I sat down waiting to see what they had to say. He said, we have trained you and you are ours. I said yes sir. He said, I love you as my own son, and I will never put you in a dangerous situation. Then he stopped for a moment gathering his thoughts. He said, the man that I work for is coming here very soon. And he might want to see you. Now I have been training you to grow, and to run this house. Because that is what he wanted. I said, yes sir. He said, if I ever flag you off of something. Do not argue with me. I know something you do not. I said, yes sir. He said, this meeting is very important for all of us. I said, yes sir.

Then he said, let's go for a little walk, I want to show you something. And we can talk more. I said, yes I would like that. So as we walked out to the back of his house, and in the woods, so we could talk. He asked, have you ever heard of a man called, Mr. B? I said, I have not. He said, that is who I work for and you will meet him. I asked, is there anything special I need to know. He said, the less you know, the better off you are. He said, he is training you to go back to his country, and be over his fields. Or to give you this house. He will ask you how old you are, do not lie. I will step in and continue your training and be your mentor. Do not interrupt an conversations while he is here. I said, yes sir. As we started back walking to the house he said, this house is now yours, and my five wives go with it. We started laughing and I said, five wives. He said, you have meet them is there any of them you would not have. I said, no sir. He said, keep the sir while he is here, drop it after he leaves. I said, yes sir. He said, do not repeat anything I have said, just wait and see what Mr. B says. He asked, how is your peripheral vision? I said, it is good why? He said, I am sure you will get into trouble talking to this man the first time y'all meet. I will stand a little in front of you. If you get into trouble I will lead you with a head nod, but do not look at me. When you are talking to Mr. B look straight at him, eye contact means everything. I said, yes sir.

As we walked back into the house he started laughing. And his wife looking at me concerned, and asked if everything was alright. He said, everything is fine, when you take Donnie home tonight give him an ounce of weed. She said, she would still looking at me, she asked, is everything alright with you Donnie? I said, yes mam, mom, dad and I were talking about business. She said, I guess it was me then, I am just feel something is out of place. I walked over to were she was setting and sat down. I asked, what is going through your mind? She said, most people and my husband would have had words by now. I looked at her and said, I have no ambition in this, I am just living life. And living one day at a time. You and your husband are teaching me things, and I trust y'all. And I am at peace with everything. All of this fell into my lap, and I definitely don't know what I am doing. So I will just follow y'all, mom and dad. He looked at his wife smiling, shaking his head no. Then he said, he really has never heard of who he is going to meet. She laughed and gave me a huge, all excited she said, now Donnie I want you to lay low for the next couple of weeks. And don't go anywhere unless you have to. We will send a car to get you and bring you over here. I said, yes mam. Then he said, you need to be taking him home. She threw me a bag of weed and said, let's ride. I said, thank you dad for everything. He said, you are good son, and I am glad. There are a lot of people that would love to be were you are. I said, yes sir, but just knowing you and mom is enough for me. He laughed looking at his wife and said, take him home before I decide to keep him over here. His wife and I walked out the door laughing. As I said, I love you dad.

On the way home she told me the rammers she had heard about Mr. B. Being in Law Enforcement when he was younger. She said, they say he is cold blooded, and gets what he wants. I stopped her and said, I was told the less I know the better off I am, were he is concerned. She said, you are right, I wish I had not heard some of the things I have. I said, I was told unless he tells me about himself it is best not to discuss him. She said, thank you Donnie, but I am so excited about meeting him. I said, yes mam. Then she said, I have heard you have become mean, are you changing on me. I said, sometimes when I look in the mirror I don't like what I see. And I wonder what happened to the real me. She said, with you Donnie, God is always there. I said, you can't see God looking at my life now. For the second time she said, you belong in a church. I said, again smiling I have tried a church once, and I add a school. She busted out laughing and said, I heard about that. I was laughing to as we pulled into my driveway. She said, anytime you need Marijuana let me know. I was still smiling and said, I will, I love you mom, she said I love you to Donnie. As I started to get out of the car she said, we will see you in a few days, stay ready. I said, yes mam and gave her a hug. I watched as she left and walked into the house.

CHAPTER 12
Autobiography by Donnie Lothridge

In a few days A strange car came pulling in the driveway. I asked my mom if I could go over to the other house? And she said yes. As I walked up to the car there were two men setting in the front seat. They asked if my name was Donnie, and I said it is. It was hard for me to understand there English. As they told me to get in the back. As I got in they said, someone very important is waiting to see you. I said, yes sir, they did not speak again until we pulled in the driveway. There were people and cars in the yard I had never seen before, and everyone was dressed in black. As we entered into the house, the guest was setting in the recliner, with a person standing on each side of him. He was talking to other people, so I looked around the room. The man and his wife was setting on the couch. So I walked over and sat down beside her. I sat and watched quietly until the house was cleared.

Then Mr. B talked to the people standing on each side of him. They were replaced by two other men. Then he addressed the man that ran the house. As he stood up, so did I and we walked closer to were Mr. B was setting. As he asked, is this Donnie Lothridge? The man that ran the house answered him and said, it is Sir. I stuck my hand out to shake his, but he turned his head and looked at the floor beside the chair. The man that ran the the house nudged his head to one side in a no position. So I lowered my hand. Then Mr. B asked how I was doing learning everything? The man that ran the house said, very well but there are still somethings I need to teach him. Then Mr. B looked at me and asked, do you know what I am? I said, you are a Mexican. Immediately Mr. B spit on the floor, and the men on each side of him drew assault pistols on me.

Mr. B asked me, why did you call me a maggot? The man that ran the house dropped his head. I never took my eyes off of Mr. B. Looking him right in his eyes. I said, Mr. B, there was no offense intended, and I do apologize. He spoke to the men on each side of him and they lowered their weapons. When I hear Spanish spoken my mind goes to Mexico. And I was not thinking of other Countries. I do apologize again for my mistake. The man that ran the house raised his head. Mr. B started smiling and said, he does have a few things to learn. Teach him what I am, and I will meet with him again. The man that ran the house said, thank you sir, then Mr. B looked at me, and I said, thank you sir.

Then there were pictures made of us as a group. Then there was pictures made of me standing with Mr. B. Then there was a picture of me made alone.

The men that brought me there took me back home. I thought on the way home how I messed things up. And if I had hurt mom and dad in anyway.

The next day there was a knock on the door, and my mom answered it. It was my other mom and she had came to pick me up. She visited with my mom for a while, and then asked if she could take me to her house. My mom said, sure, she did not see why not. So I kissed her and out the door we went. As we got into her car she said, my pocket book is in the back seat. In it is a bag of weed and some papers, roll us one up. I said, yes mam. As we smoked it I asked how much trouble I had gotten them in. She said, no trouble, I think it is great, my husband and Mr. B are spending some time together. And I love being around that man. I said, that man could kill us all. She laughed and said, I know he could, but we have to teach you what he is. I laughed and said, I thought I have already had that lesson. Laughing she said, you belong in a church. I said, that is the third time you have said that to me. She said, Donnie I mean that, God is doing something in you. And I don't know what it is, but when He is through with you, you will know. I said well right now mom I feel like I am the prodigal son. I have almost gotten shot twice over at your house. She laughed and said, both times you have not even flinched. Does it not scare you looking down the barrel of a gun. I kinda giggled and said, fear is of the devil. But it can work for you, or against you. Godly fear is a good thing. But to fear a man that can only kill the body. I would rather fear God, only He can kill the body, and cast the soul into hell.

As we pulled into her driveway she said, look at my arms. This is what I am talking about with you. See all these goosebumps, every time I am around you the power of God gets on me. I said, I see it, but why do I feel like I am fixing to get on the highway to hell. She smiled and said, I don't think God would allow that to happen to you. I smiled and said, probably not, as we walked into the house. I said, hello dad we are home. He said, you are the coolest man I have ever met. I about shit my pants when they came out with those pistols. And you did not even flinch. I said, well it had me tightening up my ass. She spoke up and said, he and I were just talking about that. Look at my arms, I still have the power of God on me. He said, I can see that. Donnie take a seat, so I can tell you about, what Mr. B wants you to know. I said, yes that would be nice.

He said, Mr. B will meet with you in a couple of days. We will come and get you. He wanted me to explain to you how he became what he is. He was in the right place, at the right time, to help with the war. And he is not a Mexican.

I smiled and said, I guess they are still pissed off about Sam Houston. Then I said, we studied in school about the World Trade International Bridge, in Laredo Texas and how people were trying to make both Countries one. But that was like the fifth grade. Then I asked, do you know how many Mexicans are here? They are saying Spanish will soon be our second language. And yes I believe they can already take this Country with out firing a shot. He laughed and said, not yet but they are close. Then he said, without the war none of what we do here would be possible. But now he has pissed Uncle Sam off so we will have to wait and see where it will end. He said, that is what he waited me to teach you before y'all's next meeting. And for God's sake don't call him a Mexican again. I laughed and said, I think I have learned my lesson on that. Then his wife said, if that is everything guys let's smoke a joint.

After we finished the joint she took me home. On the way back she said, dad is very proud of you, and he loves you very much. I said, I am glad and I love him very much to. Then I asked, if Mr. B had told them how they were doing yet? And she said, not a word, I guess he will before he leaves. And I think he would like to spend some time with you to. I said, that might not be a good thing, y'all know how to take what I say. But he is very serious about what he is doing. The Bible says to show honor were honor is due. And fear were fear is due. And that man can stand in both of those places. She went quite on me for a moment, and I asked what she was thinking. She said, about the world, and the part we all play in it. I said, you could be a hippie mom. She said, I am and you better never forget that son. I laughed as we pulled into my driveway. As I started to get out she asked, if I had any weed left. I said, yes mam I am good. Then she said, I will see you in a few days. I said yes mam. And I got out of the car.

A couple of days later I was in the yard, it was in the evening almost dark. When she came pulling into the driveway. She went on into the house and was talking to my mom when I walked in. Mom and her were talking about flowers. As mom fixed them a glass of tea. They walked into the living room and sat down. I fixed a glass of tea and followed them. After she visited for a little while she asked mom if I could go over to her house. My mom asked if I was behaving, and she said yes. In fact my husband and I like having him around, he brightens our world up like sunshine. I laughed almost spitting out the tea I was drinking, and that made both my moms laugh. So my mom said o.k. I kissed her goodbye and out the door we went.

In the car she said, go into my pocket book and roll us a joint. Reaching into the back seat I said, anything you say sunshine. She busted out laughing and said, I had to say something, I was so afraid she was going to say no. I said, I am going to get my drivers license next week. She said, I like coming to get you and bringing you back home. It breaks up the monotony, and you give me a chance to think. Before I met you again, I thought I was doomed to hell. I said, the devil would like for all of us to think there is no hope. But as long as there is life, there is hope. Then I asked, do you think Jesus was a hippie mom? Walking around preaching Peace, Love, Hope, and Joy. The only people He got on to, was the people He knew was trying to kill Him. She said, I have asked that same question. Then I asked, mom do you think Jesus Christ ever smoked weed? She said, Donnie Carroll you know Jesus Christ did not live the way we do. I started laughing and said, now you sound like my real mom. We was laughing as we pulled into her driveway. I looked around and there were no different vehicles in the yard. So I asked, is Mr.B here? She said, he is in the house waiting on us. I said, yes mam as we got out of the car.

As we went into the house her husband and Mr. B were drinking from coffee cups. And we were asked to join them, as we sat down they continued there conversation. And then Mr. B started telling them how great they were doing. And what was coming up in their future. They were very happy and I was happy for them. And Mr. B seemed to be more relaxed this time. He confirmed to me what I was told by her husband. And then he said, Donnie I was in the right place at the right time to make this happen. In this life we are all just a part of a much bigger plan. I have stepped over the line. And it is going to cost me. I do love this Country. And then he stopped talking for a moment. And said, it is getting late. Then he looked at me and said, you are my golden child. You are my gold watch on a gold chain. Keeping time of the season's and years. But your time is not yet, and you will know when it is. I am going to leave you some money for an airplane ticket to my country. When you are ready I want you to be with me. And I will put you over my field's of Marijuana. When ever you are ready to make my country your home. I said, yes sir, thank you very much. And then he reached out his hand, and I shook it and he smiled. Then we broke up our meeting. Mom said, I need to take you home don't I son? I said yes mam. So I shook hands with dad and said, thank you dad. Said goodbye to Mr. B and said, thank you again. He said, you are my golden child. I said, yes sir. So mom and I left.

On the way to take me home she was so excited, repeating everything Mr. B said to them. Then she would repeat what he had to say to me. Then she high fived me and said hell yes. I was very happy for them. We smoked a joint to celebrate. But I still knew everything was changing for me. I could feel the darkness that was around me. As we pulled into my driveway she handed me another bag of weed and said, this will hold you over for a little while. I hugged and kissed her and said, mom I still have a lot left from the last time you gave me a bag. She laughed and said good, I love you son. I said, I love you too mom as I got out of the car. Mr. B and I would meet one more time,before he left the Country for good.

I went and got my drivers license the following week. And I bought a motorcycle. I was invited to smoke some weed with some people I had meet previously. So I drove my real dads truck. When I arrived, I was asked to pull around to the side of the house, so I did. He and I smoked a joint walking towards the barn. Then we turned around and walked back to the truck. A pick up truck came flying in the driveway, pulling a horse trailer. Followed by cars, people were parking everywhere. I was blocked in so I asked him, what the hell is this. He said, we gather one time a month and have a ceremony. I wanted to invite you, but I did not know how. I said, well I am here now but I do not think I am going to like this. He said, well you can not leave until we all do. So we walked up and petted the horse in the trailer. I did not pet the horse because of what I was listening to. And the excitement that was in the air. We had formed a circle around the horse trailer. They preformed a small ceremony. Then they stuck the horse with a knife, piercing its heart. I watched as they caught the blood in a goblet, before the animal collapsed. I watched as they lifted the cup up and said more things in a ceremonial setting. Then they passed it around starting on the other side of the horse trailer. The man that had invited me whispering asked, are you alright with this? I whispered back, no I am not. I can not drink the blood, it is against my religion. He said,then you still have to pass the goblet. I watched as they mumbled something over the goblet and took a swallow. Some of them just wet there lips with the blood and then licked them. When the woman that was standing beside me handed me the goblet. I took a step back.

The man preforming the ceremony asked, and who do we have here? I told him who I was and he said, you are here and you are a part of this gathering. Now if you will not drink the blood, then you must pass the goblet. I said, yes, and took the goblet from her hand, and passed it to the man that had invited me. The man over the ceremony said, very good. And everyone was happy. Afterwards we smoked a joint, everyone got into their cars, and I left. I asked God for His forgiveness for me being there and my part in passing the goblet.

A couple of days later my friend showed up, and asked me about what happened, over at my other mom and dads house. I said, nothing has happened, what are you asking me about? He said, they say you met with Mr. B, and people see you over there all the time. And they are saying that house over there belongs to you. I asked, were did you hear this from? He said, from everywhere, people seen you in the house with Mr. B. And they took pictures of you and Mr. B together. Are you going to try and lie out of it? I said, I have never lied to you that I can remember. And yes I did speak to Mr. B, and yes there were pictures made. I said, now are you happy. He said, hell yes, that is so cool. Then he said, I have to go right now but I will be back. I said, I can see how you are going to be. There really was nothing to it. He said, right as he left.

My other mom came and got me and took me back to her house. On the way over there she said, Donnie we made a lot of people mad about you being over here. When they thought they should have been. I said, yes mam I have already heard about it. She said, dad wants to talk to you and I can already tell you what he is going to say. The house is yours, and he will continue to teach you. And nothing will change on our part. But people will kill each other to have this house. But none of them can run it, that's the reason why you were here and they were not. I said, yes mam. As we pulled up in the driveway she said, people really show there true colors when it comes to money. I said, yes mam. As we walked in I said, hello dad I see business is back to normal again. He said, it is and you can have it and my five wives any time you want it. I said, now dad are we having a bad day. No I am serious you can run this house. And Mr. B was asking about you coming to his country. I told him no not at this time, but I am going to leave that decision up to you. They are starting a civil war there and if it was me I would not go. I said yes sir, I am not going, I don't feel right about it. He said, good I like having you around. Because you are going to take this house and my five wives. I said, you keep saying that, but I can not see that far. He said, I like that about you, you are not in any hurry. I said, God has other plans for me, and then we will see. Then he said, you are set now, place your right hand on the Bible. I said, I never knew you had one of these. He laughed and said, actually it is my wife's. We all started laughing and then he made me swear that I would never grow for profit as long as he or Mr. B was alive. And I sweared to it. He said now I do not want you coming back over here until I send for you. I asked, have I done something wrong? He said, just the opposite, you have done everything right. He said, unless you need some weed, and then send one of your friends. I said, yes sir. Then I hugged him and kissed him and said, I will see you later dad. He smiled and said that you will.

Then his wife took me home. On the way back home she said, this is a very sad day for me. And I am afraid we have put your life in danger. There are people now saying they are going to kill you. I said, don't cry God has a plan. And I would not imagine, that I will stay dead very long. She said, that does not help Donnie. I said, it will be fine mom I love you and dad. This could be the reason for all of this. I am not scared or worried about any of this. It has already been turned over to God. Then I hugged and kissed her and told her I would see her later. Got out of the car and watched her leave.

CHAPTER 13
Autobiography by Donnie Lothridge

As I walked in the house that evening my world changed. Mom would still come and pick me up every now and then. But even they could tell the change in me. I started staying with my friend. My favorite song became, I am on the highway to hell. I put a pentagram on my wall. I started having nightmares and staying up day and night. My real mom had read in a magazine, that the shape of a pyramid over your bed would stop nightmares. And it did, I would cry out to God but felt He was not listening. But what God was showing me, I did not understand. I found myself going against every standard in life I had ever been taught. And the things I had judged other people of I became. I was on self destruction, and I deserved to die. My friend was the only light I had. As the wickedness grew greater, and greater.

God was teaching me things I would use later in life. As he kept showing me in the Spiritual realm what was happening. At one point I even became mad at God. Because I did not understand.

Then one day I was invited to a party, everyone that fixed me a drink put a little extra something in it for me. I had never thought about the people I ran with wanted to see me dead. Seeking power and prestige in the drug world. To them this was my going away party. Of course they had know idea of my appointment with God. And it had long slipped my mind to. On the way home everything started shifting around. So I pulled of the one lane road I was on at an old abandoned house. I stopped and parked the bike under a big tree and laying down in the driveway I went to sleep. I awoke to a shower of rain. I could hardly stand up, but I managed to get back on the bike. I thought, I am less than a mile from the house. As I drove back on the road I started tripping as the wind felt good on my face. The last time I looked at how fast I was going it was eighty. As I entered the fifteen mile an hour curve on a wet road. The bike slid out of the road, when the tires hit the grass the bike stood back up. Sending me straight into a big tree. Then all of a sudden I was back on the road again. I crossed the one lane bridge and continued up the road. Until I came to the pastor, my house was across that pastor. And that is the way I went, except now there was no motorcycle under me. I went across the pastor and down the driveway. I stopped at the steps to the back door. I could hear my sister and dad arguing about were I was. So I reached for the screen door and fell inside the house. As I got up I thought, I am in big trouble. So I spoke and said, I am home now stop arguing. But they could not hear me, so I walked around them thinking how can I get their attention. So I walked up to my dad who was still arguing with my sister. I was go to push him. But I walk through him, and his breath comes out of him, as he exhaled. He said, I have to set down, something really bad has happened to Donnie. So he sat on one couch, and my sister sat on the other. And they are quite for a while, but I am still talking trying to get their attention. And when they start talking again, I get really mad, as I slap the telephone off the bar. My sister said, well that is it for me, I am going to bed. My dad said, after that we all need to go to bed.

I think where is my body? At that moment I am pulled through the wall of the house, across the pastor, and back down the road. As I entered my body, a voice said breathe, if you do not breathe you will die. I said, I can not breathe this motorcycle is laying on me. I try to push it off of me, but I could not, then it became light and a feather. As it was lifted off of me, then the voice said, breathe. I was taken out of my body and found myself on a dirt road. I was in a line of people that was moving very slowly. We were in a waste land walking towards a moat and castle. There was a woman in front of me, and know one behind me. Then the voice said, take a look, as far as I could see now, there were people standing behind me.

It was so hot and dry know one said a word, and my tung was stuck to the roof of my mouth. And with every step, a blaze of fire filled the crimson sky. Blood surrounded the castle in the moat, and filled the ditches on both sides of the road. Fire was dancing on the blood, and with every step it became hotter, and hotter. I cried out for forgiveness, and asked God to please not leave me here. Then a clear bubble came floating down and sat on me, and I became in the bubble. It lifted me higher and higher through the crimson sky. Until I came to a great porch with huge columns, and it was all bright white. The bubble set me on the bottom step and burst.

Then I was pulled back into my body again. I found myself laying face down in the mud and water. Trying to cool my body were I was burned from the motorcycle. My head was being turned out of the mud and water. And a voice said breath, if you do not breathe you will die. So I started breathing through only half of my mouth. The other half of my face still was in the mud and water.

As I relaxed I was taken out of my body again. Back to the beautiful porch. As I walked up the steps the giant doors opened,and I was surrounded by light. In so much I could not see below my ribs. As I entered the great hallway I could hear voices on both sides of me. In languages I had never heard before. But I could understand what they were saying. As they talked about me. I had walked half way down the hallway when I stopped, and turned to my left. I then walked into the light that was surrounding a table, the length of the hallway. Behind it sat people eating and drinking. The man I was looking at stopped and looked at me. Almost like he was surprised that I was standing there. But then he started talking again as they poured some more to drink. As I looked everything on the table put off light, even the liquid that was poured. Then he stopped again looked at me and said, you have an appointment. And he pointed to another giant door. At that moment I was pulled under the door, and lay prostrate before the King of Kings and Lord of Lords. And I was unable to move because of the power, that came from the Throne of God. All I could do was ask for forgiveness. My Lord, and King said, stand up! But I said, I can not stand. My Lord, and King said again, standing up. I said, I can not stand my legs are broken. Then He came over and grabbed my leg, and shook it. Saying, now I said, stand up. As I was trying to stand two Angels came and lifted me up. But when they turned me a loose I fell back to the floor. Then Jesus Christ stood between me and God, I could stand but not very well. Then Jesus Christ asked for the book to be brought in. And it was, and my name was found in it.

I was returned to my body to breathe again. And the voice said, breathe, if you do not breathe you will die. I lay there breathing until I relaxed again.

Then I was taken back into the Throne Room of God. Where I was held up by one Angle, still unable to stand on my own. Jesus Christ said, show him. I was taken by the Angel and we stood in outer space looking at the earth. That was the size of a golf ball. From there we heard the cries of the innocent. How long oh Lord, How long, did the blood of the Earth cry out. We stood in silence listening for a while. As my mind was absorbing what I was listening to. Then we returned into the Throne Room of God.

Back in the Throne Room of God, I was told that we are made in the image of God. And as our mouth speaks so are we. The same mouth you are cussing with, you are praying with. And out of the abundance of the heart the mouth speaks. And you are praying, expecting it to come true. I wanted to show you what you keep sending up here. The highway to hell. You sing it day and night. And that is what we are hearing. I became weak and had to be held up again. Then Jesus Christ said, take him and show him. The Angel took me and we looked at the earth again. The time was during our equal rights movement. The Women burning there bras, and the Gays fighting for their rights. We could hear the whole earth, and understand everything. And we could pin point every person. There was nothing, a thought or whimper that we did not hear and understand.

I was put back into my body. And the voice said breath, if you do not breathe you will die. I still could not move as I started breathing again. Half of my face was still in mud and water, and I could tell the sun was rising. A bee keeper that lived on that road found me. But he could not recognize me, so he asked who I was. He was able to get me in his truck and take me to my mom and dads. They said, I guess this is him but we can not tell either. So they threw me in the car and took me to the hospital. They was trying to wash me up when I came to fighting, and cussed everyone out. Because of the burns. I was X-rayed and they did blood work. When the doctors talked to my mom and dad.

They said, half of his body is badly burned. His brain is swelling, but there are no broken bones. And we do not know why he is still alive. He has a mixture of drugs in his system that would kill an elephant right now. We could admit him to the hospital, but there is not a thing we can do but watch him, until he dies. So mom and dad took me home, and put me to bed.

As my eyes shut I ended up in the Throne Room of God again. Jesus Christ said, take him and show him. I was taken to a cottage and it was snowing. Everything was quite and peaceful as we stood outside a house, looking in the window. A woman and I were inside, and I was setting behind a desk. I was writing in a book and she was putting money into a box. The boxes were stacked up both sides of the walls. When she was through with the money, she went to the other side of the room and took down a box. Then she started taking out bags of Marijuana and putting them on my desk. Then a young woman came in that had two young children with her. They were bare foot, and not dressed for cold weather. She said she would like to get a front on the Marijuana. The woman working behind me came to the front with a book in her hand. She stepped up beside me and opened the book in her hand. She showed me she was three thousand in the red and we could not go any farther. I looked at the children a gave her some of the money, that was laying on the table. I said, now this is for the children, for clothes, shoes, and food. Then I gave her a bag of weed, and said this is for you. She started crying and thanked me, and out the door she went.

The Angel and I stood there for a moment. Then the Angel said, that is what is wrong with this. Then I was taken back into the Throne Room of God.

I have thought about that all my life. And weed has surrounded me all of my life.

As I entered my body again laying in my bed The voice said, breathe, if you do not breathe you will die. I lay there in severe pain unable to move or open my eyes. My body was cold and every joint hurt. My face was on fire from being burned so badly. I could hear my mom reading the Bible to me. The book of Isaiah, I thought that was funny. Here I am going from earth to Gods planet , and she is reading a prophetic book to me. I tried to open my eyes and speak but I could not. Then I tried to just wiggle a finger, but I could not. Then I realize my brain was unhooked from the rest of my body. A voice said, this is what it is like to be in a coma. Your body is asleep but your mind is not, and it wakes up from time to time. I thought about the people in hospital's that was fixing to cross over, the things they listen to before crossing over. Then I went out again.

As God brought me back to his house, I stood with an Angel again before Jesus Christ, and again He said, take him and show him. This time the Angels took me further into the future.

I was outside a store across from the White House, I had a bull horn in my hand, and the Spirit said speak. I said, You my Lord have to speak I don't know what to say. Then as the Spirit spoke I spoke. The Spirit said, just like Satan because of your multitude of trade, you have been weighed in the balance and found wanting. You have become a whore, and the stink of the earth rises into Heaven. Just like Solomon you are, and your kingdom will be destroyed.

I am arrested and taken to Guantanamo Bay in Maryland. I will probably be there three years according to the growth of my beard.

Then bombs destroyed everything, and few others and I come walking out. Standing at where the side of the building was, is a man dressed in black robe, with a hood that covers his head. He says follow me, as we walk back toward where the White House was. I trip and fall over a dead man, looking at him I say, what a waste he never knew You God. As I tried to stand He takes me by the arm, and in a flash of light we are gone. Into Heaven, and I am home.

As I entered into my body again my mind awoke, and I was not breathing. The voice said, if you do not breathe you will die. I had to fight inside myself to breathe this time. When I had my air back and was at ease the voice said, there is one more place we will show you. Then there was silence and I was floating, not exactly in my body. I was in the middle of two worlds.

Just then my mom walked into the room, she was followed by an E.M.S. lady. My mom watched as the lady put the ointment on my face and chest. The lady said, he is burned very badly. My mom said, I have talked the fire out so he can rest. The lady said, I have known people that could do that, but I can not. Mom said, some people say it is witchcraft, but everything I do is from the Bible. And she told her the story behind it.

As the E.M.S lady put the ointment on my face the pain return. I was cussed her out but know one could hear me. I guess because of the pain I went out again. I was taken back into the Throne Room of God.

This time God and I talked and He said, what you say you breathe life into. There is a place I would like to show you, and after that you will come back here. The place is called outer darkness. When God finished speaking there was a great fear that fell upon me. I fell backwards and threw the floor. Into a place of total darkness. A place of emptiness. And a place without God. We all have God's power living inside of us here on earth. It is something we are born with. I never realized that until I was there. The emptiness of this place, a place of floating in black, black, darkness. Like lying on your back in bed, with no strength to move.

As I floated there was these little light spirits that kept coming by me. They were making this sounds as they talked to each other. I watched them for a while, until the being all alone set in. As I spoke they stopped, and then more stoped. When there were fifteen or twenty gathered around me. They attacked me with there teeth and claws. The pain was so great I wanted to die. As they cut me with there claws, and bit and chewed on my flesh. And when I had screamed, begged, and cried all I could, it would stop. Only to start over again. I went through this seeking and crying out to God.

Until the voice said, if you do not come to the light, you will wander through darkness forever. I said, if only I could find the light. That's when a little speck of light appeared. I thought if only I could go back into my Father's house. I started moving very slowly at first towards the light. And the closer I got to the light the faster and faster I went. Until I was pulled into the light, and then it was as if I was pulled across outer space and time. Until I was back in my Father's Throne Room. Were we were all talking, including Satan. My Father said, It is time for you to go back. I said, I don't want to go back, what if I am not able to come back and be with You. He smiled and said, I am not through with you yet. You still have work to do. I said, what if I don't make it back. He smiled again and said, you are coming back. Then as I was starting to fade Satan said, it want be long and I will see you again. I said, don't hold your breath you old nasty serpent you.

And I returned to my body.

CHAPTER 14
Autobiography by Donnie Lothridge

As I lay there thinking of my experiences with God, and wishing I could move. Hearing my mom coming into my room and reading the Bible to me. Still leaving my body but not going to Heaven now. I was going to a place in the Spirit realm between Heaven and Earth. A place that has been talked about by the prophets of old. And I believe it was the reason why the lost sea scrolls were left out of the Bible. It is a realm of dragons that surrounds the earth. And I do not think they are evil. Satan is chained in the Throne Room of God, in the form of a Dragon. But did God curse all dragons, I don't think so. When I would leave my body now I would go to this place. And watched time, and time again, as the dragons circled the earth. It was a place of peace and harmony. There are a lot of things in God's world I will never understand. There was a piece of furniture in God's Throne Room that moved and had eyes all over it. And when God moved it moved. The only thing that came to my mind was Ezekiels wheel with in a wheel. I am so glad I am a child, and God is my Father. And yet Jesus Christ called us His bride, and little god's. We can do nothing on our own. All I can say is this, God's Love lives in all of us. And the after life is no joke. So when everyone of us stands before God, and we all will. To be Judged by the Word, the Blood, and the Water, were will we stand. If I considered a step, a day, when God had me on the highway to hell. After five steps I could not take it any more. And in this life, that is the life we live, I am one day closer to where I want to spend eternity, than I was yesterday.

About that time mom walked into my room with the E.M.S lady. She had came to put the ointment on me again. Mom said, she would make a cup of coffee for them, and left the room. As she rubbed the ointment on my face, my eyes open. She smiled and said, I see you are awake, can you speak. I said, yes mam I think I can. She said, we have missed you, were have you been. I said, I have been with God how about you? She said, if you have been with God then tell me something about me that know one else knows. Giving my spirit a chance to change I said, I thought you were going to ask me something hard. Then I said, your first husband you think about all the time. She said, I do. And you will leave who you are married to now, and go back to your first husband. A big smile came across her face as she said, let me get your mom. Before my mom could come into the room my eyes shut. They both had a cup of coffee in there hand. And mom tried to get me to open my eyes but I could not. Then the E. M.S. lady said let me try, she shook me and said, Donnie Carroll open your eyes! And my eyes opened but then shut back. They were just open long enough for me to see my mom.

I could hear them talking and laughing. As the E.M.S. lady told her she thought I would have a long recovery, but she believed I would be fine. Then she said, push him, get him out of this bed and walking as soon as possible. Feed him soup and give him water to drink. To keep him from dehydrating. Then she said, I have to go, my husband will now come in my place to see about him. And mom seen her out, and then return to my room. She sat in a chair, opened the Bible and started reading it to me. Then she stopped and asked me, now what did you say to her Donnie? Then she started back reading.

The next time I come to myself my mom had me propped up on pillows. And I was eating chicken noodle soup. I remember asking her, how long have I been out of it. She said, four days since the bee keeper found you. Then I asked her, who is all these strange people? She asked, what do you remember? I said, God, Heaven, and Hell, You and the E.M.S. lady. Then she asked, what did you tell her? I said, she asked, where I had been, I told her with God. She said, tell me something only God knows, so I told her. Then I said, I am going out again.

When I came to this time dad was dragging me to the bathroom. My arm was around him and I was trying to make steps. But basically he was holding all my weight up. It took me about a week for me to be able to walk, and then it was baby steps. And then they would lead me around by my hand and feed me. My brain and my body was not connected, and it seemed to be getting worse than better.

One day we were at my mom's, sister's house. I always looked at the floor and never raised my head. My dad grabbed me by the hair on my head so I looked into his face. And it totally struck me wrong. That night when they put me in bed and left the room. I said, alright God it is time we had a talk. You have brought me so far, and I pray and believe that You do not intend on leaving me like this. Please God don't leave me like this touch my mind, and help me to go back to normal. Help me God in Jesus Christ Name I pray. At that moment it was like a billion explosions going off in my brain. And lights flashed all in my mind that hurt so bad. As God was waking up my mind. And it lasted all night as my body shook from the pain.

My mom took me to our family doctor and he examined me. He held my head up and said, look at me Donnie I want you to think. Then he asked, who am I? I looked at him for a moment. Then he asked me again, who am I. I said, you are my doctor, and called him by his name. He laughed and said, that is right. Mom and him had been over everything that I had been through. Then he said, time is what he needs now. And I think he will be fine. Just keep working with him and bring him back in a month.

On the way home I asked mom, why does my brain go to sleep and then wake back up. She said, it's because of everything you have been through. And it will take time to fix it self. I smiled and said, God and I are working on it. (What If?)

Then my mom said, I thought we had lost you Donnie. I said, mom how can you ever lose me, when we are both in Jesus Christ. And I had to do this, you have heard me say before, I had an appointment with God. She said, that does not help the pain. I said, no mam, but mom this is a road we will all go down. And the only question is were will we spend eternity, and nothing else matters. I have already heard what they say when I talk about were I was. They laugh saying, I hit my head to hard. When they die let them tell me that, on the other side. Mom said,

Donnie they don't know what they are talking about. Mom why has serving God became the greatest battle of my life? That made her laugh as she said, it's the prize waiting for us at the end of this life.

As I got stronger mentally and physically, I started going back out again. And I started running with my friend again, but he could not see the spiritual war going on inside of me. Or how God was going to use me. And he helped me pull it back together. And I started going back over to my other mom and dads house. My other dad asked me, what I was going to do about what had happened to me. I laughed and said, that is why we have laws in this Country. He laughed and said, you know thats crazy right. I laughed and said, God loves crazy people. At the time I said it, I had know idea what I was going to do, or what I had even said. He said, this house is still yours. I said, thank you dad but now I have something else to do first. He said, Donnie revenge is no way to live. I said, dad do you think I want revenge, I am not interested in revenge. I am following God, and I have know idea where I am going. We smoked a joint, I told mom and dad I loved them, gave them a hug and left.

Later I met a man that had been a P.O.W. a military Ranger. And he had two other military friends with him. We were riding around drinking beer and smoking weed. I could feel the aura he was putting off, as he explained the bulging scars, he had all over his body. I asked him if he was a Christian, and he said most definitely. The man driving the car had been shot across the stomach with a machine gun. He said, he maned the machine gun in the helicopter, and worked rescue missions. He was a Christian also, and so was the man setting on the passenger side.

We had pulled in a lite up parking lot to take a piss. When we started to get back into the car, a man came around the side of the store hollering at us, with a gun in his hand. We all turned around and looked at the man. The Ranger said, I have this men. The helicopter man said, don't you hurt him. The Ranger said, I am not unless he is extremely stupid. Then the Ranger said, you need to stop and we can talk. Then the man raised the gun in his hand. The Ranger said, yep he is that stupid. The helicopter man said again, don't you hurt him. Then he said to me, don't blink if you do you will miss it. In less than a second the man with the gun, was now laying on his back, with his own gun sticking into his mouth. The Ranger asked him two questions, how stupid are you, and are we having fun yet. Then the Ranger as they talked took the gun out of the mans mouth. Took all the rounds of ammunition out of the pistol and gave it back to him. As we got back into the car the man that had never seen combat asked. Were you serious when you said, I could blow your brain's all over this parking lot and not lose an ounce of sleep over it. Helicopter man spoke up and said, it's not our job anymore. The Ranger in the back laughing said, thank God. Then we picked back up our conversation. The only one that it seem to change was the man asking the questions. We rode around and partied for hours, then they took me back to my truck. I thanked them for their service and sacrifice for our Country. And for the education they had given me. We all laughed and hugged each other and I left.

CHAPTER 15
July 20, Page 4

Next I met a girl, and you know it's always about a girl. And we did the hippie thing. Had a child and moved out of state.

But before we left I took her to meet my other mom and dad. As we talked we smoked weed and she listened. We talked about Mr. B, and what was going on in his country. And we talked about my house there. He said, it will always be here for you. And it is yours when you get back. They gave us a bag of weed, even though I did not want it.

So on the way back home, she was quite. I asked, what is wrong. She said, while you and I were talking before we moved in with each other. I had heard a lot of things about you, but I had never believed them. I said, yes mam. Then she asked, how deep are you into this. I said, I am not deep at all why. She said, it sounded to me like you know Mr. B. I said, I do know Mr. B. She said, it also sounded to me like you own that house. I said, if I want it, it is my house. She said, so we can move into that house, and they can move out. I laughed and said, we have plans in another state. She said, but we could have that house. I said, Love there is so much to that house, that you don't understand. That becomes your life, and that stays your life until they take your ass to prison. And we have a child now and so it goes much deeper than just us. Then she asked, you are going to remain a drug dealer right? I said, that does seem to be my reputation. She said, good I love weed. I said, how about we move and start over. And put all this stuff behind us. She said, I don't believe you can. Everywhere you go someone will know you. I said, well other than some smoke every now and then, I would like for us to live a normal life. She laughed and asked, what is normal for you? I laughed to as she said, yep what I heard is true. I said, you don't understand. She laughed and said, oh well.

The next day we moved, two days later a drug dealer showed up that we both knew. We were still unpacking but we invited him in. We set in the living room and smoked a joint. He asked, if we were looking for anything and we said no. Then he said, this is my territory and if we needed anything let him know. We said we would and he visited for a while and left.

She said, yep Mr. Donnie two days, two days, it looks like a normal life to me. As time passed I started driving a tractor trailer on a chauffeurs license. It was before it became federal regulated, I also ran into a branch of law enforcement, that asked if I would become one of them, and work for them. So I was sworn into that branch of law enforcement and worked for them. We worked narcotics for a little while until the day two people were killed. We talked about the options that were available, and I said I would go back home. My girls had already left. The rest of this is Government.

So I came back home, and it was a mess around my parents house as I was unloading the car. Two deputies came up and picked me up and took me to a house to be sworn in. The Sheriff said, raise your right hand and repeat after me. Because there is no way you are bringing that shit up in here. So I was sworn into local law enforcement.

After that I went to find my girls, I found her and put her into the car. She said, I don't know why you came and found me, we are through. I said, look in the dash and roll us a joint. As she did I turned down a dirt road. We both got out of the car and lit it. As we smoked it she said I hate you. I said, well I love you. She said, I will never stay with you now. A county car pulled in and turned around. She said, more of your friends I suppose. I said, it's not what you think. She said, you being a law enforcement was fine with me. But after what happened Donnie there is no way I can live with you. Then she started crying and said, two people are dead. She said, we are hippies Donnie that is what we are, and I can not do this. I asked her were she would like for me to take her. She said, to take her back to were she was. I said, I will not do that pick another place. Then I asked her, where is our child she said, she is safe. Then she told me where to take her and I agreed. On the way over there she started crying again and said, I don't hate you.

But I just can not ever live with you again. I said, well I love you. She said, I want ever tell anyone. I said, you were in the wrong house to tell me that. How much do they know? She said, not everything. I said, how about I love you. She said, if I say that then you will change the way I feel right now. I said, I am leaving I can not stay here. She said, good I don't want you around here. So I dropped her off were she wanted to go and left.

The next day my dad asked, what the hell is going on? I said, it is a long story. He said, it better be a good one, I seen your girl and she looked like she just came out of a car wreck. I said, I did not do that, some other people had her, and she was brought back to me like that. He said, you know the Sheriff and I are cousins. And he tells me you are a law man, and a deputy of this county. I said, it's true my cover is I lived in another state. He said, it's a little late for that son, her dad has already been here. And he said, while you were putting her, and her stuff in his car. Your girl and a another man were begging you not to kill this mans brother. I said, yes dad it is true and two men are dead. About that time a county car pulled into the driveway. A deputy got out and said, we moved your folder to the city. He said, if anyone ever asked, you were born in the city, and raised in the county. I said, I might be moving. He said, I thought you might be. Dad and him talked for a few minutes and he left.

Dad said, that might be the best thing until we can put a lid on all of this. I said, I don't know what I am going to do, or were I am going to go. He said, you are the only man I have ever met that pisses in one hand, and shits in the other, to see how fast one of them will fill up. And then he said, I love you, and he gave me a hug. Saying I am glad y'all are alive. I said, thank you. He said, stay here at the house until I can come up with something.

The next day my uncle showed up. He said, your dad told me your situation, and I think know matter what happens, take that baby with you. I said, well uncle no matter what I do now, it will not turn out good. My life has been nothing but trouble, and I don't have to look for it. It has a way of no matter what I try, it finds me. And I don't know how I am going to survive, what will I do with a baby. Here she has family on both sides until I can get back. He asked, would you like to tell me what happened. I laughed and said, so dad did not tell you. He laughed and said, I am not saying, but I have heard enough. Your dad and all of us are x military, and thought you might want someone else to talk to. So he sent me. I laughed and said, I will give you the short version. We moved to another state and I became a Truck Driver. I entered law enforcement, my girl was beaten, my cover was blown, a drug deal went bad, two people are dead, and my girl would like to know. Where the hell her man went! And when she looks at me, she thinks about what has happened, and she is a hippie.

He said, sometimes bad things happen, and people get killed. She may never get over it. But the living keep on living. And from what I have heard you have already died once. God is dealing with you Donnie and if you can't see that, then something is wrong with you. I do not proclaim to be a Christian, but I can see it. You will keep on losing everything until you get it right with God. Then I asked, do you know what God wants me to do. He said, I have no idea, but if moving is not it. God will definitely let you know it. I said, thanks for the encouragement, and we laughed. Then I hugged him and thanked him for stoping and spending time with me. As I watched him pull out the driveway I prayed, asking God to never stop working with me, and to help me get it right. And until I did get it right to put a hedge of protection around my family and I in Jesus Christ Name I pray Amen.

As I walked back in the house my mom said, I just got off the phone with your cousin. He said, he would help you get back on your feet. I said, thank you mom I will do it for a little while, but I do not think it's a good idea. She said, It is the only one we have now. I said, yes mam.

I moved out of state and met the Sheriff a couple of times. He was as country as the day is long. And I liked to listen to him talk. My cousin taught me how to be a plumber and tried to keep me busy. I picked up another job at a metal plating company, and moved out. I kept looking to God wandering were I belonged. And hurting for my girls. I would call my mom one time a month. To find out how everything was with them. I felt I was only existing not living as my life was empty. A store owner were I stopped at every day asked me if I had ran across a big air compressor. He said, he had one stolen but no one had any leads on were it might be. I said, an air compressor that size would be hard to hide, and I knew were one was at a shop.

And that is all I said, two nights later a man walked in the plant where I am working, and hit me in the back of the head, with a piece of half inch galvanized pipe. I am toting thin pieces of three feet long pipe to be re-plated. As I hit one knee the pipe I am carrying fall onto the floor. Except for one piece that I have with both hands, that is now pointed at him. He is behind me but I can see him over my right shoulder. He is preparing to strike me again, and I am preparing to ram that piece of pipe through him. As I spin on my knee I set my other foot and leg to push off the floor with. Other people in the plant is coming towards us so he turned and ran out the door. One of the two men he entered the plant with, was coming right towards me, with a knife in his hand. So I started walking towards him whirling the piece of pipe in my hand, my eyes were set, my mind was blank. As I was rolling the piece of pipe I was carrying over the back of my blood soaked hand. He ran into a corner of the plant, and pulled some carts we used, between us. As I walked up to the cart, still whirling the piece of pipe. I said, I think there has been enough blood shed for tonight. As I could feel the blood steady dripping of my hand. I could see the man was panicking, So I said, killing you for something he done, just don't seem right to me. But tell him I will now be hunting him, and it does not matter to me where I find him at. Also tell him I know were he lives, and I will be over there later tonight, to decide whether I am going to burn his house to the ground or not. Did you hear what I said, I asked? Almost crying he said, yes sir, yes sir I did and I will tell him. I said, good now get the hell out of here before they catch you. And like a rabbit he ran out of the corner of the plant, down the lane and he was gone.

I put my hand to my head to feel how bad the gash was. One of the women there said, he hit you with everything he had. I said, I believe it I am blind in my left eye. Another woman said, we all hid when those men came into the plant. I said, you did right. Then she said, you need medical attention, I will call nine one one. I said, no don't do that, I don't want this on a scanner. I will drive myself to the police department, and then to the hospital. I said, If you would be so kind as to call, and tell the boss l am going to the police department. They asked if I could drive and I said yes.

At the police department I gave him my information and told him I was going to the hospital. He said, good because you are bleeding all over my floor. He said, another officer will meet you at the hospital to take your statement. I said, be sure he brings my credentials with him. As I started to leave I say be sure you tell that piece of shit the next time I see him he is fucked. The officer started laughing and said, I did not hear a thing.

At the hospital they put seven stitches in the back of my head, and told me I had a concussion, but I should be fine. And my eye sight should return in a few days. The officer took my statement and returned my stuff. He and I were laughing as he said, don't do nothing stupid now. I asked, you mean like riding out to his house, and doing donuts around it. Hoping he is stupid enough to give his location in the house away do you? Now officer you know I would never do anything like that. He started laughing and asked, you're not looking for a job are you. I said, not at the moment, but I am thinking about taking a little ride, would you like to go with me. He said, I would love to but I have other things to do. I laughed as I got into my car and took a little ride.

A couple of nights later at the motel room when I was just about asleep. God spoke and said, in three days there is a man coming to kill you. In a flash I was on my knees beside the bed. I said, you are God and if You say it will not happen, then it will not. God said, you have not learned anything yet. I said, I have Lord and will start talking to people about you. Another voice said, you can run, just run away, you don't have to stay here. I said, I know the story of Jonah, and if I leave now something much worse will over take me. So I will stay here to meet my God. God then said, he will not kill you.

The next night at work my mom called the plant. She said, last night while I was praying for you Donnie, God let me know something bad is about to happen to you, and you need to come home. I said, yes mam I will leave in the morning. I returned home and was reunited with my family.

I was in a depressed state of mind, but God and I were working it out. I walked the hallway in mom and dads house day and night talking to God. And when mom would get up at night and have a cup of coffee, before she started reading the Bible. She would fix me one also, I would stop walking and we could talk. She had read the Bible from cover to cover many times. And she was my sounding board for some visions, and prophecy.

Tonight she said, Donnie you know you are going to walk a hole in my floor. I stopped pacing and sat down beside her. I said, I am sorry mom but God at this point in my life, reveals Himself to me this way. I am stuck on prophets that made a three day journey. Jonah had a three day journey to Nineveh, but he made it in one day. She said, Donnie, God would show me things when I was young that I could not understand. And so I asked Him to take them away. People would have thought I was crazy with the things God was showing me. But I am not you, I have never died, nor have I ever been in law enforcement. I said, mom I have to do this, God and I are walking it out, and I don't know how far it is to were I am going. She said, well I can see you have already taken it to the Lord, but I want you to do something for me. I asked what is that mom? She said, I would like for you to go and see a psychiatrist. I asked, do you think there is something wrong with my mind? She said, no but I do think you have been through a lot. I said, yes mam I will go and see one. Then she said, Donnie make sure what you are doing for God, is God. I smiled and said, you always say that mom. She smiled and said, and I always will.

So I got back in the Spirit realm and started walking again. And she started back reading the Bible. I walked until day light and went to bed. As I lay my head on my pillow God showed me a man that I had known for a very long time. He had fire coming out his eyes, ears, noise, and mouth. I awoke and immediately hit my knees. I prayed not that I doubt You Lord God, but I doubt me. If it is true show me again. And I seen the same thing again. So I asked, Lord show me one more time not that I doubt You, but me. And the same thing God showed me again.

CHAPTER 16

Autobiography by Donnie Lothridge

As I lay awake thinking about the vision, and how that man and I rubbed each other the wrong way. Then I fell asleep for about an hour. I awoke to the sound of my mom moving around in the house. I sat up on the bed and thought I need to tell mom. I got dressed and walked into the kitchen were she was preparing dinner. I said, mom I need for you to set down, there is something I need to discuss with you. She said go to the table and sit and I will fix us a cup of coffee. I said yes mam, and set at the table. She took a seat at the table, and we started to talk. We sipped on our coffee as I explained how clear the vision was. And that I was shown three times. She said, you do know that he is with the fire department. I said, no mam, I did not know that. Then she said, all I can tell you is make sure it is God. I laughed and said, you always say that mom. We set and visited for a little while, and I talked to her about taking the stitches out of my head, and she said she would. Then I said, I think I am going to see dad at work. She said good it is about time I got out for a little while.

As I rode over to our family business. I was singing a little song to God just enjoying the day I was in. Then when I pulled up at our store, the doors locked on my car. And I could not get out, so I asked, o.k. God what is it? It shocked me when God said, he is in his store across the road, go over there and talk to him. For some reason I said, I am not going, send someone else. God said, I am sending you. I said, now God you know that man and I do not like each other. And I am not going. That's when God said, there is no one else, and you are going. Then God caused a conviction to hit me in the stomach, and it rose to my throat cutting my air off. I fell over in the seat of my car choking to death, whispering I will go Lord, I will go.

God turned me loose, and the doors unlocked, and I got out of the car. I said, alright God, but You are going to have to do the talking, I don't know what to say. As I started to cross the highway my dad came around one of the buildings. He asked, ha Donnie were are you going? I said, I have to go see this man across the highway for a minute, and then I will be back. He laughed and said, I sure hope God is going with you, you know that man does not like you. I kinda laughed and said, I don't think we have to worry about that part of it.

As I entered the mans store he was standing behind the register. To the left of stepping inside the store. He asked, what are you doing in my store boy? I said, I came to see you. He said, you have seen me, now get the hell out of my store. I said, there is a little more to it then just seeing you, I have something to say. He said smiling, say it, then get the hell out of my store. His friends that was setting at the bar said, we want to hear it to Donnie, and we will even buy you a beer. I said, maybe later guys, what I have to say is personal between him and I. The store owner said, come here, lean over the counter and tell me what it is about. I did and whispered, it is about God. He said, hold it right there. Then he told the girl that was working in the store with him. You have the store, Donnie and I are going outside to the burn barrel.

As I held the door open for him he laughed and said, you must be crazy as hell, if you think I am going outside in front of you. As I walked outside I asked, were would you like to have our talk at. He said, just go around to the right of the building and keep walking until I say stop. I said, yes sir. When he told me to stop and I turn around, we were about ten feet apart. He looked at me and said, talk. I asked him when was the last time he talked to Jesus Christ? He said, I accepted Him as a child and I have never looked back. I asked, do you know how much He loves you. He said, His presence has been on me for two weeks now, and I can not shake Him, as he started crying. I said, you are not going to shake Him, God is here, you here, and I am here. Let's make it right, right now. He said, I can not, I have been drinking all day. I said, I really don't think that matters at this point. He said, I will tell you what I will do, I will stop drinking right now and when I get home tonight. My wife and I will kneel in prayer at the foot of our bed, and we will rededicate our lives to Jesus Christ. I started crying and said, I don't know that you have that long. He said crying, I have to, I will not go to God drinking. We hugged each other crying, and I told him I loved him. He said, I love you to. I said, don't let this pass by you. He said, I want and thank you Donnie. As I walked off I looked back and said again, don't let this pass by you.

I walked back across the highway, got in my car and drove home. God turned me loose in my parents driveway. And I realized I never talked to dad. As I entered the house I hugged and kissed mom. She asked how dad was. I said, I don't know when I showed up it was all God. She laughed and said, I can feel Him. Then I told her I was going to bed. I needed sleep. She said, I will wake you when your dad comes home. I said, thank you. My dad asked, what had happened to me. All I could say was, it was the power of God.

Not very long after that the fire department was called to a brush fire. Or what they thought was a brush fire. And there was a scarred electrical cable. When the man from the store pulled up in a new fire engine. He parked on the scarred line. Realizing the situation he tried to move the fire engine, and everyone else back. Not knowing the fire engine was grounded because of the water, and charged with electricity. When he approached it, it pulled him to it like a magnet, killing him. And they said, it was just like the vision God had given me.

I did not attend the funeral, but years later I ran into his wife. I was at my cousins house smoking weed, and she came in looking for her son. She started to leave and then stopped, as if she was thinking hard about something. Then she turned to me again and said, there is something I need to tell you before I leave.

I asked, yes mam? She said, that day you talked to my husband at the burn barrel. I said, yes mam I remember. She said, that night when he came home he was not drinking. And he and I, at the foot of our bed rededicated our lives to Jesus Christ. And he never touched another drop till the day he died. I just thought you should know that. I said, praise the Lord. She smiled and said, thank you. I said, it was not me but God that talked to him that day. She said, I can feel God now. I said, I know. And she turned and out the door she went.

There was a family reunion not long after the fireman had passed away. And my spirit was being steered by the Spirit of God, and I was seeking God about it. And I was talking to mom about it. Her answer was, you and God, are on a different level than most people. And I am not going to enter fear with that. You and God have to work it out. But I am going to tell you what I always have, make sure it is God. She always made me laugh as I would say, you always say that. And you always say pray about it. She said, sometimes you scare me, with how you are following God. I said, mom it's like I am looking straight at God, and He has me hold it until it's His timing. And then I am going to blow up if I don't let it out. This last time mom was the strongest, as God flowed all through me. But it became easy after God almost choked me to death, and I surrendered to Him. She thought that was so funny, I had never seen her laugh like that before. Then she asked, why is death your thing? I said, it's not always about death. God does not want any of us to perish mom. We look into death for Salvation, and none of us leaving this earth without crossing over, you know that. She flashed her eyes at me and laughed. (What If?)

My mom asked me if I was going to the family reunion with them, I said, no mam. I told her I would be down later after everyone had left. I did not much feel like being around people. I showed up after most of the people had left. And the land scape had changed. I spoke to one of my cousin as I walked by him. He was setting in a rocking chair outside under a pecan tree. He said, Donnie everyone is getting old and passing away. I said, it is true. Then I cut our conversation short because of the Spirit that was on me. So I asked if we could talk later, as I walked to the barn. I looked across the field first, and then the sky. I was looking and feeling for God. Could the Angels still be here, or did they leave with grandpa. Could it have been his prayers or the Spiritual wells he dug. I asked myself what I was looking for? God has not changed I thought, so why am I here? I picked up a small rock and threw it out into the field. I asked myself again why am I here, and what am I looking for.

As I turned walking towards the house, God's Spirit spoke to me saying, you have somewhere else to go. I knew my cousin setting in the chair would be next, to go be with God. As I got close enough to talk to him, the Spirit said, he knows. He spoke to me but I said, I have somewhere else to go, I will see you later. As I turned walking back to my car the Spirit said, turn not to the right or the left and salute no one. At that moment I knew were I was going. As I pulled into his driveway I said, this is all You God, I don't know what to say? As I knocked on the door I was invited in. My aunt sat at the table and asked if I wanted a beer? I said, no thank you I came to see your son. He and a friend of his was playing, slapping each other around in the living room. I noticed what he was watching on the television. The friend of his said, I have to go anyway but I will be back latter.

As his friend left he asked me what I wanted. I told him what he was watching was an abomination to God, but Jesus Christ loved him very much. He turned about three shades of red before lighting into me. And said, this is hell, and there is no God, we have been put here to suffer. I said, there is a God, and there is a hell, and some of us are living closer to it than they realize. He jumped up and slung the door open, saying you get the hell out of my house and do not ever come back. As I passed through the doorway it was slammed behind me. The Spirit rose up inside of me and said, I knock the dust off the souls of your feet as a testimony against this place. I never looked back, there was nothing else to do. In a couple of days I was taken to his sister, she was walking down the street. As I pulled over I said, Lord God it's all you. I rolled the passenger window down so we could talk. She said, Donnie Carroll I love you so much, and I hope you have not come to talk to me, the way you did my brother. I said, I have. She came around from the passenger side of the car. I rolled the window down on my side of the car, and said, please listen. She said, I can not hear you Donnie. I said, I wish you could. I tried to talk again, but she said, there was a wall between us. I said, I wish there was not. Then she kissed me in the mouth and said, I love you Donnie. Walking away from the car she said, I can not listen to this. I said, if only you could. They both died in car wrecks. I think he died first.

The Power of God is Almighty and it is not about us, but God living in us. John the Baptist said it this way, God must increase, and I must decrease. And there is another scripture in the Bible that goes like this. How can two walk together unless they be in agreement. Since I know God will not change, what will I have to do to allow God, to change me. Father, Son,and Holy Ghost. What If? (What If?)

CHAPTER 17
July 22, Page 4

I am going to skip a few years. What you have read is who I am.

Now my dad and I are setting around talking one day. And he asked me why did I not go on the road truck driving. He said, I think you have driven through the worst of it, and now that the teamsters strike is over with, it might be a good carrier for you. I laughed and said, you have lost your mind, there is nothing on that highway but trouble. He said, I know you have seen what martial law looks like, and a few dead people. But up north or out west is where the money is at. The south will always be the south, it's a good place to retire. But you are young and have been all over this Country. I said, I think I can smell what you are cooking. He said probably not, this will always be your home. I said, I might try that just to see, and I believe like you, there are a lot of good people in the world. But so far my opinion of the world is not very high. I am from Missouri now the show me state. I said, I don't think you have been where I have been, or seen what I have seen. I said, but we will try it your way, you are right there are no jobs here. To make good money here, I will have to grow weed, or run a drug house. And that will be only until they decide to bust me.

So I went on the road and started talking to people making friends. I ran into a man that was a law man, he and I was running together through the northern states. We were talking about the American, Mexican agreement like everyone else. We both had our guard up. But at the same time we trusted each other. I was also friends with other law men in a few states. Back then the Federal Government was doing everything they could to control the trucking industry. And I got to noticing everyone would be driving crazy, after the man I trusted and I would part ways. So I started writing down tag numbers. I was friends with a law man back home, that knew I was in it to, and I would get him to run the license plates for me. He said, boy you have some serious Federal problems going on. I laughed and said, at lest I know who they are.

So the next time I run up on him, I asked him if he is trying to get me killed. He said, hell no just trust me. I said, that might be what the problem is, I do trust you. So we have been following each other, every time I would make a run up north, he would pick me up. When all of a sudden I am surrounded by cars that are pushing on me. He asked me, do you see these cars? I said yes, I can't help but see these cars. He said, follow them and do what they say. I asked, are you sure you are not fixing to get me killed. He laughed and said, just follow them. So I followed them to the back of the White House, and they had me park my truck. Now I don't know how many of you have ever been interrogated. But being strapped to a chair naked, is not my idea of having fun.

When I came to the first time I was threatening to kill everybody. As I was asked about tunnels between the U.S.A. and Mexico. I was also asked about my dad. And I went out again. The next time I came to. I was asked, are you a law officer. My reply was yes, and I gave the town I was deputized in. He said, no you are more than that. I said, yes I am a Law Man, and gave him the state. He said, give me your badge number. I said, because of the work I done, you can not access my files that way. It takes a phrase. He said, give it to me. So I did. Then he told his first officer to pull my file. When he came back into the room he said, the information he gave you is correct. And I went out again. Except this time I was kinda in la la land, I could hear and feel things that was done to me. Including pictures or images that was put in my mind. Including one of the men there saying, bring him to my house when he comes to.

When I came to, I was back in my truck, and they said, you have seven chips put into your body. And I felt like I had bathed in motor oil. As I set there I felt depressed. I was asked, what I thought about what I had been through. My reply was we are talking about our Government. They could have asked me and I would have said yes. I don't mind being tracked. They said, don't feel bad about it you are not the only one. And we were not talking on the C.B. I think today you would call it a halo, and the Bible would call it the Beast.

The same thing happened when I pulled my truck around the White House to be parked. I could hear them clearly, and they could hear me with nothing in my truck being on. If you are not hooked up to this thing don't get excited and think you want one. The Bible calls it the Beast for a reason. (What If?)

They said, let's go driver there is somewhere else you need to be. So I back the truck and trailer down the street. And turned it around at the cross roads. As we rolled down the streets they spoke to me on this halo. We know your thoughts and we can promise you, we will put this truck wherever we want to. I laughed and said, I am not a rebellious child. But every now and then I am from Missouri. They said, the truth is we don't know what to do with you. I laughed and said, just love me like Jesus Christ does. They said, turn right and go up this driveway. The four lane was blocked in front of me and there was two cars beside me. I said, like I have a choice, but it would help if I could swing wide. They said, you don't need it we have watched your driving. I was still drugged and did not fill well at all. As I pulled into the lower driveway to the house. A man came walking down the hill from the house, and I pulled the air brakes out on the tractor. I watched as he was still coming down the series of steps, that was made in the hillside from the house. He came around the front of the truck and walked up to my door.

He asked, may I help you. I said, well sir, I don't know, I could be lost. He laughed and said, I hear that a lot. He said, get out of the truck and let me take a look at you. I said, yes sir and climbed out of the tractor. I staggered trying to get my feet under me. He started laughing and asked, are you alright? I said, yes sir I think so. He said, good you should get better in a little while, are you alright to drive? I said, yes sir from here I am going home. He said, home for the weekend. I said, yes sir. He said, I do not want to interrupt your plans. But I do need to take some pictures of you, and this beautiful truck. I said yes sir. He said, and polite to, your mom and dad raised you right boy. I said, thank you sir, as he took me by the arm. Showing me were he needed me to stand so he could take the pictures. After that he gave me a piece of paper with numbers on it. He said, do not lose this, you will need it later, and I think that is everything for now. I looked at the four lane highway, and asked if he was going to back me out into it. He said, take a look we own it, the road was blocked again and he said, that is for you, go on. I thanked him, and climbed back into the truck, backing it out into the highway.

The ride back to the south was pleasant, and we started talking on the c.b. again. They told me it would take a few days for my body to stop excreting the oil. And I could expect my hair to become baby soft. I thanked them as they escorted me back home.

I told my mom and dad what had happened. My dad said, if it was the Government you should be fine. He laughed and said, they live in your world, crazy as hell. We laughed and I said, I think I will quit driving. He said, that is not the answer. I asked, do you know of a better one. Then he rubbed my hair and laughed saying, I believe your hair is getting softer. Then he said, you could go into the military. I said, with my back the way it is from the motorcycle wreck. I don't think I could pass the physical. He said, no I think God has other plans for you. And I can honestly say I have never met anyone like you. I don't even know why we have a television any more, all we have to do is watch you.

So I kept driving and went up north again, the group I normally ran with asked, when you see him are you going to kick his ass? I said, no, but I am not going to say, I have not thought about it. They laughed and told were he wanted to meet me at. We had a meeting with some other men, and when they asked me what I thought about it? And after I told them he said, Mr. B. I said, it's not because I back him, but I believe in what he said. And why do I want to help build a country up to overthrow this one. When there are other countries we can help. He said you can not stop this. I said, I am not going to try to stop it. I am just saying for me to participate, I have to agree with it. And I don't agree with murder, kidnapping, or any of the other bull shit going on over there. And as far as I know, I have never smoked a tourist. And I hope I never do. They said, I guess we know were you stand. I said, you do.

After everyone had their say, he and I talked some more. After everyone had left he asked me what I was? I said, I am a Christian just like you. He said, after viewing your life I am glad I am a Catholic. I laughed and said, we both believe Jesus Christ is the Son of God. He said, I still don't know what I am going to do with you. I smiled and said, just love me like Jesus Christ does. We got back into our trucks and left. As we left I thought, I hoped he realizes I am a Law Man, and I am not going to get caught up in any of this bull shit. Some one picked up on my thought and said, he does. I reached for the c.b. and realized it did not come from there. Then I thought about the space ship how we talked with our minds. But I had a band on my head then. There was no band on my head now. I could hear people laughing then. And someone came on the c.b. and said, under these circumstances why don't we do this the old way. Someone else said, that would probably be best for everyone. And I could feel the power on my brain less. Then I was told that I would be left like this unless I was getting into trouble. Then they would let me know about it. I said, yes I understand. The next few times I ran up north. I would always hear on the c.b., I bet you want to kick my ass. And that would make me laugh.

At the next gathering we had I was asked about an officer that said he knew me. And he was from the south also, and I was asked why this man hated me. I said, I do not know who this man is. My friend said, he claims he knows you. And he has stalled out mine and your plans for right now. He said, you and I will slow down until I find out what he is up to. I said, thank you, l am cool with everything, long as it stays cool. He said, I will flag you off if it does not look good. I said, thank you.

The following month I was working on something for our Government. As I rolled up the road a man came on the c.b. he said, leave what you are doing alone. I said, thank you. As I got closer to what I was doing. Another man came on the radio and said, they are fixing to make you the main drug hauler for New York City. I don't know your business just thought I would let you know. I said, thank you driver. As I got a little closer someone else came on the radio and he said, make your delivery. And set as normal but don't touch that money. If you do they will frame you, and you will pull one hundred and thirty years. I said, thank you I have already been warned. He said, we will talk latter. I said, thank you.

I ran everything as normal, and set as normal. A man approached my truck and said, I have what you are looking for. I said, I don't know what you are talking about. He said, I have your money. I said, you have the wrong truck, and you need to get the hell away from this one. He said, I need five dollars. I said, I would not give you a dollar if I had it, now get the fuck away from me. And I cranked my truck up. As he was walking away from my truck, he looked back twice, and scratched his head. Then he went between some buildings, and I pulled onto the highway. All hell broke loose as I was accused of embezzlement. Since I knew, that they knew, I did not touch it. I said, fuck y'all and headed for the south. Then they said, I just embezzled thirty two million dollars of a branch of governments money. I laughed and said, y'all all are fucking crazy. As I pulled onto the interstate thinking, do you really want to play this game. My trailer was empty and the Peter-built I was in wanted to run, so I dropped the hammer.

The halo said, don't get my people killed. I said, yes sir these cars were made for speed, but they cannot run long distances at high rates of speed. I ran that truck up to triple digits and held it there. As I watched the escort drop off of me. A little after dark I slowed down, because I was out running my headlights. I was still pushing eighty five to nighty miles an hour. When I started around a truck, he held me in the passing lane. The blond in the truck took her shirt off, and she was pregnant. We talked about a minute when the power of God hit me. I said, I sure hope your not holding me out here for a reason. Then I prayed with no response, so I called on the God of Abraham, Isaac, and Jacob, for my deliverance from the hands of these uncircumcised philistines. And the Heavens opened and I said, because I am fixing to put this old Peter-built in your lap. He said, we would not. And there it set a tractor trailer in my lane with no lights on. I just jerked my truck hard to the right and then to the left. The other truck went off the road, and I could see the blonde girl bouncing all over the cab of the other truck. I picked up the radio and asked if they were alright. They said, yes but we have to clean the shit out of our pants. I laughed and it dawned on me, at the speed I was traveling, to the object in the road. There was not enough time or space for me to avoid hitting it. I started shaking, crying, and praising God for my deliverance. (What If?)

CHAPTER 18

July 24, 2021

Autobiography by Donnie Lothridge

From were I was at, I kept seeing town lights and thought there must be a road that cuts across here somewhere. And I had a feeling I needed to leave the interstate. So I took a road that turned into a gravel road. And dropped my trailer. I came back to the interstate and drove a couple of more hours. The sun was coming up and I drove to a town, where I knew the Law Enforcement. I parked the truck and got out. As I went in side he was glad to see me. He said, I knew you were coming here. I asked, how is that. He said, hell boy I have been hearing about you for two days. I said,really. He said, you ant the first driver that ever had a surprise waiting on them. The funny thing is my wife and I were just talking about you. I laughed and said, I do my kin that way. If I want to see them I just start talking about them, and they show up. He said I have a question for you Mr. Bandit? I smiled and said, yes sir. He asked, how did you make it around that other tractor and trailer? Still smiling I said, I am glad you asked that question, so you can tell your wife. I just set behind the wheel, Jesus Christ does all of the driving. I really did not make it around it, I went through it. He laughed so hard, and said, Praise the Lord. She definitely will get a laugh out of that. He said, I guess you want to use the telephone? I said, yes sir I would like that. About that time a another law man, stuck his head in the door and said, I have all three of them here. The Law Man I was seeing said, I will be right there and stood up, and so did I. As he walked passed me he put his hand on my shoulder. Saying go ahead and use my phone Donnie, laughing he said, or Mr. Bandit. As he was walking out the door he said, I always knew I would see you again.

Then he stuck his head back in the door and said, when you get through come out here. I said, yes sir I will. I called mom and dad's house, and dad picked up the phone. I said, just the man I want to talk to, how would you like to see your son alive again. He laughed and said, I would like that very much. I said, well you might need to come and get me. Then I told him what town I was in. He said, I will be right there. Then I said dad, you might need to bring a gun with you. He laughed and said, I kinda figured that. Then I told him I loved him, and he said, he loved me to.

As I walked through the doorway the Law Man was pacing the floor talking. The other law man was leaning against another doorway. And three people was setting on a long bench. He said, well Donnie here is what we have. These two black guys were best friends, until she came into the picture. She was a white girl. He said, and I know there dad's. Now I have had to lock him up for thirty days for shooting at him. And then I locked him up for thirty days for shooting at him. Now she is the only one I have not locked up yet. And she is the one running back and forth between them stirring up all this trouble. I am wandering if I locked her up for thirty days, if these two want work this out and go back to being friends, before somebody gets killed. He said, I have them in here now on charges again. But I am thinking about locking her up this time, what do you think. I said, yes sir, it sounds to me like locking her up is the only avenue you have not tried yet to keep the piece. He asked, so you would lock her up for thirty days? I said, that would be a lot better on her than standing trial. For conspiracy to commit murder. His eye brows raised and he asked, that carries about thirty years? I said, yes sir it can. Then he looked serious at her and said, lock her up. And let the other two go. She started crying as the law man was reading her the Miranda Act.

Then the other Law Man looked at me and said, let's walk outside Mr. Bandit. I said, yes sir. As we walked out the front door he asked, did you call your dad? I said, yes sir he is coming to get me. He said, that will take him about two hours. My wife is fixing dinner, why don't you come and eat with us. I said, I would love to but it will take me that long to clean my truck out. Then I asked, by the way were would you like for me to move it to. He said, just leave it right there, I am going to fine the hell out of them for parking it there. He and I laughed as he said, when you leave lay the keys on my desk. I said, yes sir. Then he asked again, are you sure you want come to the house for dinner. I said, yes sir, I thank you for all you have done for me. But I need to get ready to go home with my dad. He said, O.K. take care of yourself Donnie. I said, you to sir. And he,left.

I cleaned the truck out, and my dad showed up. As we were riding home he said, you know you can talk to me if you would like. I asked, if he had a joint? And we started laughing, and I said, I guess I owe you an explanation. He said, no you don't. I said, well it was all government and they tried to kill me this time. And I have been framed. Supposedly embezzlement. It was supposed to be a drop that never took place. I was warned about it when I started towards it, by the government guys I have been working with. All I can say is it was all government. He made a funny little laugh and asked, how much was it for. I said, thirty two million dollars. He said, someone does not like you, and has marked you. I said, they told me he is a short pecker wood from the South. And they say he is Law Enforcement. He asked, do you know him? I said, not yet but I will. I asked, you don't mind if I lay low around the house do you. He said, you and I both know I don't mind, and when we get home you can help me throw the television out in the yard. I laughed and said, you have told me that before. He laughed and asked, if I had a joint. That made us both laugh. Then he said, I hope one day you write a book. I said, one day I might. Then he said, I can honestly say, you are the only hell you're mom has ever raised. I laughed and said, but it's not the devil. Even though he does get over on me sometimes.

My mom and I had a very strong bond, and that bond was God, the Father, Son, and Holy Ghost. But she tried to never get in my business. And if I asked her something, her answer was, I will pray about it. A few days after I was home she and I were talking about how God used her on the radio. And how God continued to work through her. She looked at me for a moment and said, Donnie if you are looking for some insight from me. You have came to the wrong person, I am not you. And I have not gone through what you have. I try to keep you in line with God, then set back and see what God is going to do. She said, you do venture far away from God sometimes, but He always brings you back. I said, mom It's like I am left alone until God can use me again. Some people looking at it would call it back sliding. But I never forget who God is, or what he has done for me. It's like God has shown me all these roads I would go down. The people I would meet and those I would reach. I thought every Christians life is like this? And to be honest with you, I am kinda getting use to this world throwing me out of it. She said, son I don't know what I am going to do with you. I said, mom after every time God can use me. Satan shows up and carries me out into a desert. Were I am taught about demonic spirits that are pushing and pulling on me. And I fell miserably, over and over.

But I am learning about the spiritual realm. The good and the bad, and without my Lord and Savior, I am nothing but dust. And mom when my truck went through the other one, it was like I was no longer there. But in my subconscious mind I could feel and see the material pass through me. And the Power of God was so strong. The driver that held me in the passing lane said, you know you did not make that. I said, I know.

My mom and I was quite for a moment and then the phone rang. As she picked it up I could hear the man from the house they took me to, after my interrogation. As she said, he is standing right here. As she passed the phone to me, she walked in the kitchen. Put both hands on the sides of her face and said, no, no, no. Looking at me she said, if you take this job they will send you back on a slow train. This is not you, or who you are.

The man on the phone asked if I was ready to go to work with him. I said, not at this time my mom was not well. He handed the phone to the man I trusted. He said, hello Mr. Bandit, now don't you go getting all sanctimonious on me. I started laughing and said, I would not believe in doing something like that. But we are all called to live out different parts. He said, you are a mark just like me, and that is all you will ever be. I said, that might be true but my mom is sick right now, and I think I will set at home for a little while. He said, then I will be seeing you around. I said, most definitely. Then he hung up the phone.

My mom busted out crying and said, I know you will be killed if you take this job with those men. I said, don't cry mom I want take the job. She grabbed me and said, you promise me. I said, mom I am through, if I haul anything it will have a company seal on it. She said, you promise me. I started laughing and said, I promise you mom.

I started reading the Bible at night, and God started showing me what was ahead of me. Angels with drawn swords, and my life hanging in the balance. I asked God if I could avoid some of these roads. I think all I did was make Him smile.

The next week my dad said, you have to do something besides just set here you have to live again. He said, do something even if it is wrong. What he was saying, grow weed, get a hobby, do something. He knew how much I loved to watch it grow. And it does require a lot of time. So I started growing, and the plant's looked really good. About two months into it I remembered a vow I had made to two men. So I said goodbye to my plants and destroyed them. I told dad I was going back on the road. He said, you need to talk to your mom before you do that. I said, yes sir I will. (What If?)

The next morning I awoke and got dressed, I walked into the living room. My mom was setting on the couch reading the Bible. I fixed a cup of coffee and sat down beside her. I said mom, I think I am going back on the road. She asked, if I could not find a job close? I said, mom that ant trucking. She said, I am just afraid something bad might happen. I said, mom I serve God more on the road than any other time. I praise Him at sunrises, and sunsets. And I pledge an allegiance to our flag and country. I said, mom there is still some things I need to look at. She said, please be careful. I said, that is what the C. stands for in my middle name. She laughed.

So I went back on the road I ran up on my old group and we started talking again. I was setting in a truck stop talking with my window down to another driver. He said, see that man in that silver car. I said, yes I see him. He said, that is the man that is wrecking your world. I said, this is the first time I have ever seen him. He said, well he claims he knows you. I looked at the man again and said, I may have seen him somewhere before. But I have been all over, how could I remember were I met him at. He told me who he was, and what he was. I laughed and said, we may have crossed each other somewhere. What is he doing this high above the Mason Dixon Line. I said, he looks like a movie star, but with more hair. He busted out laughing and said, I would not tell him that. I said, well now I can put a face with the trouble. He said, it did not come from me. I said, it never does. He asked, what are you going to do about it? I said, I am going to try, to stay out of his way. He said, if you stay out of his way, you will be better than most. I said, and if I can't I will cross that bridge when I come to it. He said, good luck with that driver.

Then he asked how I made it around that other truck. Laughing I said, I did not make it around it. Jesus Christ was driving the truck, I was just holding on to the steering wheel. He said, I hope He stays with you, your going to need Him. Then someone came on the radio and said, if you want play the way we want you to. We will do a reverse and pile busts on you, up to thirty two million dollars. I laughed and said, I hope you don't mind if I put a few of my own on there. Hell all I have ever seen you do is nickel and dime. The driver setting in the truck beside me said, shit driver you are going to get us both killed setting right here. Then he said, I am going to ease on out of here. I said, I will wait thirty minutes and then I am to. And see if I can get clear from this sack of shit. He said, I hear you on that one driver. And he pulled out of the parking lot. Thirty minutes later after listening to more bull, I left to.

Two states higher in the country I was picked up by a beautiful blond woman. On the c.b. she said, good morning Mr. Bandit. I said, good morning. She said, we are high enough in the country to talk. I said, girl you are an Angel. She said, not really I work for the devil. I laughed and said, how can I help you. She said, by helping me keep you alive. She said, our job is to keep you out of trouble. I said, yes mam. You do realize trouble finds me, I don't have to look for it. She said, yes and do not yes mam me again. She said, you are tagged, and someone has made a terrible mistake. I said, why because there are two of us. I have ran up on him before, and we do look alike. She said, you are smarter than I thought. I said, to many people know me to be something I am not. And I thought he had left the road. Then I said, don't tell me there is another one. She said, I don't know but I can tell you this. Around you there is a big mess, and it's like a big ball of yarn. I said, I can feel you. I feel there is a big cat, that likes to bring me out when they are bored, just to slap me around. That made her laugh. She said, you will see me from time to time, if you stay out here, and I will

126

try to help hide you. I said, yes thank you Angel. She said, don't call me Angel, I work for the devil. I asked, what do I call you? She said, you don't. Then we were quite and she was gone.

I was out driving about four months this time, during that time there were several big bust that they put on me. But Washington was listening to what I was saying about the American Mexico agreement. But there was a senator that was killed in a rest area across the interstate from were I was sleeping. Helicopters and the law enforcement was everywhere. They woke me up, and I handed the officer my drivers license. He said, hell Donnie we know who you are. And we know how to find you if we need you. I answered his questions and he moved to the next truck.

I ran the rest of that week, I also seen the blond Angel again. She said, they are fixing to run you out of trucking with a wanted poster. I asked for what? She said, she did not know, but it was to try and protect me. I told her what I thought about it. She said, it may not happen, but that is what she heard. She was right, I was told that they had a wanted poster on me. And if I did not stay off the hill for the next three years, or until the American Mexico agreement was through. They would activate it and I would go to jail. So I told them I agreed, and I would stay off the hill. For the next three years.

So I went home, I told mom and dad, I was not staying long. And I would be moving out. Law Enforcement came and picked me up and took me to a bust. And asked me some questions about it. Then they brought me in again. The man that was working it I loved very much. He was let out of prison to work it. I hugged and kissed him and asked if he wanted some help. He said, no he had this. I said alright then I would see them latter, and they took me back home.

A couple of nights later I went into town to see some old friends. There was a couple of women there that know one seem to know. When we were getting ready to leave they approached me. One of the women asked if my name was Donnie? I said, that depends on who was asking. She said, a friend had given her my name. She said, she had just gotten out of the hospital a month ago. She was about to lose the house she was renting. And she was tangled up in a drug bust. People had already been killed. And she was scared to go to sleep at night. And she just wanted out of it all.

I said, girl I don't know how you got my name. Or who your friend is, because I don't ride a white horse. And I could be in trouble myself. Now if you are looking for someone to run with. I can do that. But if someone wanted you dead, chances are you will be dead. She said, I just want to move and start over. I said, we can do that but it will take time. I need to get a life outside of the one I have now. And I don't know how this is going to work. But we can drop below radar for a little while. So I found a job on a dairy, and I found out she was a witch. And I thought that was funny, and she and I lived on the dairy for three years.

One day I seen a man at a barbecue house, that my family knew. And I told her my parents are fixing to show up here. She said, she would be very happy to meet them. I said, they will be very happy to meet you to. My dad stopped at the owner of the dairy first, to find out were I lived. And he told my dad it was my day off, so he would not be interrupting my work. As they pulled in the driveway I went outside, and was very happy to see them. And hugged and kissed my mom. Then she punched me in the arm and said, that was for not calling me. Then she punched me again and said, that is for not wrighting me. Then punched me again and said, that is for all the gray hair you gave me, thinking you might be dead. Then my girlfriend came out of the house and hugged and kissed my mom. Mom said, on the way down here I was thinking about whipping your butt to. For not making him do right. We all laughed as we hugged and kissed dad to. He opened the trunk of the car and said, there are three years of Christmas in here. I said, well dad we haven't gotten y'all anything. He said, you don't have to, we thank God we found y'all.

As we walked into the house and sat down, they asked us how everything was? We said, everything was good. The money could be better but we were surviving. Then they asked me what happened? I told them I had put them through so much I just had to get away. My dad said, that is what parents are for, to try and help. I said, I understand that, but I kept y'all's house torn up all the time. And trucking is the greatest place for me to talk to God. He said, tell us what happened the last time you were out. I said, I seen the man that is destroying my world. A Senator got killed across the interstate from were I was parked asleep. They put a wanted poster on me, and said, if I came close to Washington D.C. They would have me arrested. And I was called out to a drug bust and was brought back in. Dad laughed and said, I heard about that. So why hang around there and bring y'all down. If anyone was looking for me I was not there. I said, I love y'all, I don't want to bring this down on y'all. My dad said, that is also what family is for. I said, now that my three year's is up, I wander what they are going to do next. I said, you know this could give someone a bad attitude. My dad said, more than that.

Then my dad asked, my girlfriend to tell her story? She told him she was tangled up in it to. But that she loved me and wanted to stay with me. And that other than the first time we met. We had not talked about it. That I just stepped up to the plate, and we had been together ever since.

My mom and dad were very happy, that we were happy. And we ate, and laughed until they left. I told them as they were leaving not to tell anyone, that they had seen us. And they said, they would not.

After they had left she said, your parents are very nice. I said, they are. She said, your mom knows I am a witch. I said, she does. She asked, will she not like me because of that? I said, no we have witches in our family. She asked, can I meet them? I said, one day you might, but until then you are my little witch. We ran around inside the house playing, and found ourselves laying on the bed. Then she asked, why have we never talked about you being in law enforcement? I said, it is apart of me I keep hidden. She asked, are you on the run? I said, no mam I am not on the run, and nether are you. She asked, are you working on anything right now? I said, no mam, but sooner or later they will call on me again. And I have taken an oath to serve this Country. And when people are being robbed, threatened, and killed. That's were I come in at, to try to give them something else to think about. She asked, has anyone ever tried to kill you? I said, yes mam they have. She asked, why does law enforcement act like they are your friend, and then throw you to the wolves. I said, it could be they are hoping you will fit back into society. Or it could be you cut into somebody's money. But if they can not control there animal, they need to put it in a cage. And I do know what it feels like to be hunted, and trapped, and the feeling of drowning.

My grandpa said, that is when Jesus Christ will come walking to you on the water. She said, well your God and mine are not the same. I said, yours might have let you drawn. She hit me playing and said, that is not funny. I laughed and said, my God has never been late. Then she asked, me had I ever killed anyone? I don't think I ever answered her question. I said, after three years of being here, people are learning were we are. And I can feel the grass growing up around me. It might be time for us to move.

She asked, tell me more about what you do? I said, I will give you an education. What does controlled substance mean to you. She said, someone is over it. I said, it is supposed to be controlled with public safety in mind. She said, now I see. I said, in that world nothing is as it seems to be. And they will turn it to protect themselves. She said, but that is not right. I said, so you are looking at the greatest mind fuck ever invited by man. I said, they call good evil, and evil good. She asked, why don't you go into law enforcement full time. I laughed and said, I have worked close with people before. And I had a bad experience. I said, look on the door of our law enforcement cars. She said, I know the star is upside down. I said, right. (What If?)

She said, I wonder how we got into this mess. I said, we were put here by a Beautiful God, to try and make a difference. Peace, Love, Hope, Joy, Long Suffering, Gentleness, Kindness, and Mercy. Now that is the Attributes of my God. And us being a Christian should reflect these.

She said, I like that even though mine and your God, is not the same. I said, I don't know what I am going to do with you. Laughing she said, just love me. I said, I can do that. She said, you better. Then she asked, tell me about Mr. B. I froze like a cat and said, he was a supplier of Marijuana. And you and I know smoking Marijuana will not kill you. So I try to leave that alone. The people that use me go after the powder, and weapons. And from what I heard, what you set up was all of them. Heroine, Cocaine, and Weapons, so you did good. She got all nervous like she was thinking about it again.

So I started talking about Mr. B I said, I met him three times and he taught me about growing Marijuana, and running a drug house. I was supposed to go to another country and be over the grow. Or I was supposed to run the drug house for him. The man training me flagged me off of going because of the violence in that Country. I was killed by other drug dealers because of the house. Then when he got busted they came and got me to run the house. I asked, what had happened? All they would tell me was he stepped over the line.

Two months later I was picked up and taken back to the house. I knew both the men whose car I was in. They said, Donnie we would like to show you something. When we pulled into the driveway, I started laughing. They said, look at what a mess this is. I said, what we have here is a Wild West show.

As we pulled up a man in the yard started cussing me, trying to get the pistol out of the holster. I said, try the one on the other side of you. You might have better luck. As we pulled on through the two men in the front seat are rolling with laughter. Then they said, you caused all of this. How long do you think this is going to work? I said laughing, if he don't learn how draw one of those pistols. Only until someone shoots his stupid ass. That started the men in the front seat falling over with laughter. On the way back to my mom and dad's house, they told me they could not run that house. And asked if I would take it. I told them I could not, I was flagged off of it by dad, and I was told never to come back over there, know matter what. I said, that was before they took dad away. I said, the only other thing to do would be start a new house. And I will take there business. He said, we can't do that. I said, then this is over, we all started laughing again about the man with the gun. Then I said, think about what I said. He said, I will but there is know way it can be done.

CHAPTER 19
July 26, Page 4

We started looking around and found a job in another state. She asked, how do you keep going. I asked if she was alright? She said, I am fine, but I never knew you could just live on a farm the way we do. I said, yes mam out of sight, out of mind. She said, so this is the way you go under. I laughed and said, Mexicans have been doing it for years. Then I asked her, how long has your family been in this Country. She said, I never thought about it Donnie, how about you? I said, I am half Indian, half German, with a touch of Irish. She started laughing and I said, the German part was illegal during the civil war they say. And I am not against anyone wanting to come into this Country. She said, I am the happiest I have ever been, why is that. I said, it could be God, or it could be you have learned how to turn loose. And only live in the world you are in. Not thinking about what is in the world. Living the simple life.

We moved on a farm. We lived there for two years without any trouble. But then one day, a man showed up, and pulled a rifle on me. And he threatened to kill me. I interrupted him and said, you talk to much, and I have things to do. I said, either shot me, or get the hell off this property. Or give me the rifle, and I will show you how to use it. When my girlfriend came out of the house because of him yelling at me. She asked, what is going on? When he seen her he threw the rifle into the seat. Put the truck in drive, and slung gravel all over me. I said, there goes a man with to much money.

She said, it looks a lot like what we are trying to stay away from. I laughed and said, you are getting smarter girl. You are starting to spot the clouds before they get here. Then she started getting upset and said, all this time I felt safe with you, but I don't know if I can take this again. I said, girl I have been poisoned, killed, shot at, and threatened, so let's look at what is coming. She said, you are crazy you know that. I said, if I get mean it's to stay alive, or send someone to meet their god. Now if you want to go home, go ahead. She said, no I want to stay with you. I said, if they fire me then we will know. She asked, know what. I said, ask for a raise because they will keep you own. And I will stay here and work. Because they know you can't do it alone. I said, I am going to start growing Marijuana. She said, they will see it. I said, I hope so. She asked, why does it not feel so bad when I am talking to you. I said, if you knew how dangerous this is you would not say that.

So they fired me and gave her a raise. I kept her amused growing Marijuana. One night she and I was smoking a joint and she asked, now what are we waiting on? I said, you will see if it happens.

We went to town one time a week for groceries. She and I had watched cars being busted, coming through town. That day as we came out of the grocery store, a Law Man walked up. He said, hello Donnie how are you today. She grabbed me by my left hand and was squeezing it. I shook hands with the Law Man, and said, fine how might I help you. He smiled and said, I have noticed you watching some of the bust going on in this town. I said, yes sir I was telling her what was going on. He said, did you see on television where a branch of government has declared bankruptcy. I said, no sir we have not seen that. He said, yes and we can not let that happen. I laughed and asked, are you running for office next term? The Law Man said, I am. I said, well you know this is not the way to get back in office. He laughed and said, you let me worry about that. I said, yes sir what are we going to do about it. He said, I will send for you in the next day or two. And we will talk about it. I said, yes sir. He said, thank you Donnie. I said, thank you Sir.

As we got into the car and started back to the house she asked, is this were Law Enforcement pulls you into it? I said, this is were we try to save their dumb asses. And no, right here is were you learn what will get you killed. She said, I do not understand. I said, I am in Law Enforcement working now with another Law Man. But you never take anything they offer you. She asked why? I said, it is a paper trail that leads other people, to your back door. Then I asked, were you looking for a payoff on what you were working on. She said, it would have been nice. And they threw me to the wolves. I said, if you do something like this, you have to have the right motivation. I said, you grew up in a rough neighborhood. And over the years you watched most of those so called bad asses. Get killed or put into prison. Now we don't mess with weed. You smoke it, and its gone, and it is good for you, like medicine. I said, now we have to play there game. Call the boss start a fight and leave. I said, that is what they done to me. She asked, were will we go. I said, to mom and dad's.

In a couple of days two plane cloths cops showed up. They asked if my name was Donnie? I said, it is. They said, there is another officer that would like to see you. I said, let us get a shower and we will be right there. So we got in the car and started up the road. She asked, how should I act? I said, be yourself that is the best part of you. Just don't say nothing about us growing. She said, I hope they ask me, I am going to tell them. I said, you crazy girl you had better not. She started laughing.

As we pulled into the officers yard we were met by other officers. He said, follow me to the office he is waiting. We said, yes sir and followed him in the building. When we came to his office, he was setting at a desk. He said, I know you have been watching me pull cars over, and making bust. I said, yes sir we have. He said, some of them have been big busts, but that is not the main supply. I said, no sir it is not. They took my girlfriend into another room. He said, I want to know how and were it is coming in at. I said, I have no idea I work on a farm. He asked, then you want help me? I said, I did not say that, are you sure you want to do this? Because I thought you wanted to talk about it? He said, I do and I am asking for your help. I said, alright you are thinking it is coming in by the highway. He said, it is coming in by the highway. Then he swore me in and when I turned around, there was a another officer standing behind me. He said, hello Donnie what are you doing here. I said, trying to help the Law out. He said, after that last bust you were involved in. I heard you were down here growing Marijuana and laying low. I said, I was but the Law had other ideas. We looked at the Law Man, and he was in the state of shock. We both busted out laughing as the Law Man said, well I see you know each other. The Officer said, I have known him most of his life. And I know his family they are good people. I said, thank you. He asked, is she with you, I said, she is but this is the first I have heard of a safe house. He said, I think it would be a safe place for y'all to go. I said, you know I have already turned down one. He said, no I did not. I said, it is nothing against you, and you know that, but how safe are they? He said, well if you don't take it what will you do. I said, live life the way I always have. He said, well I can't make you go to one. The Law Man hung up the phone and said it was all set on the safe house. I said, we can not except that, we looked at her and she agreed. I looked at the Law Man and said, you don't have very long. The Law Man said, I can not protect you if you do not take it. I said, we will be leaving the State in a few days. Then the Law Man thanked me and we left.

CHAPTER 20
July 26
Page 6

On the way back to the house I said, we need to call dad and let him know we are headed that way. She said, I hope they like me? I said, they do just don't practice any witchcraft in mom and dad's house.

I had my operation, afterwards when I was well again, I took a job logging. Driving a truck and operating heavy equipment. And we got our own place. I was still praising the Lord, and she was still into her dark arts. I loved her very much, and it would get pretty weird around the house sometimes. But I would not say anything, because I knew if I did, she would just say don't ask. So I let her do her own thing and be herself. We were happy and she would ride with me sometimes.

I asked her one day to ride with me because I thought I would spend the night out of town. She and I checked out the tractor and trailer and we made a run to the woodyard. We came back and picked up the second load. As we were going to the road out of the woods there was a curve. That had a dipped out place in it. When we turned the fifth wheel broke and the load shifted. As the load was turning over, the tractor twisted standing it up on it's back tires. All we were looking at was the sky. As the tractor started to come back down, leaning to her side, her door came open. I reached across to her and yelled, take hold of my arm and make a ball. As she did, I had the steering wheel in one hand, and she had a death grip on my other arm, above my wrest. I drug her up on the dog house in that cabover Peter-built tractor. As the tractor came crashing to the ground, her door slammed shut. And now she was setting on the door. I asked if she was alright, she said, I

137

think so all but my arm, I think it's broken. She was sitting in a ball position on the door, and I asked if she could stand up. I reached my arm across again to help her up, but the seat belt had tightened against her. I unsnapped the seat belt, while she was saying. If you don't get me out of this piece of shit of a truck, I will stomp your ass. Then she took my hand and stood up. Her legs were week, and she was shaking, as she fell back against the top of the truck. Smoke was coming in the truck with us, and she asked, is this thing on fire? I said, no mam that is antifreeze, can't you smell it. She said, I can now. She started to crawl out though the windshield and I stopped her. I said, this is a two piece windshield, your half is busted out. But mine is not, if it turns loose while you are trying to get out, it will cut you in half. So I kicked my half of the windshield out.

She crawled out through the windshield and stood up. I was still setting in the driver's seat as she asked, can you get out? I said, I think so and unsnapped my seatbelt, not thinking that seatbelt was holding me. I feel onto the door were she was. Laughing at me she asked, are you alright. I said, yes I am fine, and crawl through the windshield. I did not realize my back had been cut all the way across it. She said, oh my God you are not o.k., the back of your shirt is soaked in blood. The boss showed up and said, take my pickup and go to the hospital.

She has one of the bones in her arm broken. And I have a half inch torn place across my back. They put a cast on her arm. The doctor talked with me for a minute and says, I could spend an hour or more putting stitches in your back. Or I could just cut the tare place off and let it heal up on its own. Then he took a pair scissors and cut it off. We were released from the hospital, and go home.

That evening about dark my boss showed up, to pick up his truck. I walked outside and he asked if we were alright? I said, yes sir we are, she has a broken arm, and I have a very painful cut across my back. And we killed the hell out of the Peter-built. He said, yes y'all did, but don't you quit on me. I will pay you for a couple of weeks, then I will come back and see you. I said, yes sir thank you. He said, if you or her have any problems go back to the hospital. I said, yes sir we are both just shaken up. He said, it's called trauma. I said. yes sir.

As I went back in the house, she was working on a hippie project of hers. She stopped and asked, why is death always around you? I started laughing as she continued, I have never met anyone like you. I said, I thought I lived a normal life, leaning into God. Then she started laughing and said, you know I could have been killed. I said, yes mam you were at deaths door. But God saved you, I was not thinking about anything I was doing. I was just reacting to what I was looking at. And the thought of part of you, or all of you having that truck laying on you was not a good thought. She said, when I looked and the door was open, I thought I was gone. I said, me too. We both were crying as she said, I don't guess we should talk about it. I said, no we should talk about it, cry about it, pray about it, and give thanks for it. She said, you are right, I will never forget it. I said, yes mam.

In a couple of weeks a new tractor pulled in the yard. My girlfriend and I walked outside, and she said, shit. My boss said, come on Donnie I want to show you something. I looked at her and she said, go on its your job. I climbed up in the Auto Car tractor, and we road around the block. As we pulled back into the yard, she came outside again looking at the truck. He asked, do you think you can handle it. I said, I was thinking about quitting driving these big trucks altogether. He said, I know but I can not let you quit on me. I don't want ether one of you to quit on me. I don't want that hanging over me, you are to good of a driver. So this is what I was thinking, both of y'all get in the truck and take me home. Then ride around and get familiar with the truck, and go to town and buy some groceries. He handed me some money and said, and be on the job Monday. Now let's go I have things to do. So we did what he asked.

As we road around I said, at least this one has a hood on it. And we are lower to the ground. She was all up tight, as I was checking out how it leaned without a trailer. She kept talking about how she was scared. I told her the trailer turned us over last time, because of the fifth wheel breaking. And yes you were almost killed. But this was the best way to get over it. Then I ran up on a dirt road and said, alright your turn to drive. She said, I am not driving this truck. I said, you are driving this truck, you drove the other one, you can drive this one. She said, but everything is different in this truck, and I have a cast on my arm. I said, so I will help you change gears. She said, you are crazy you know that? I said, God loves crazy people. Now come on and drive. As we switch places she said, alright big truck you ant killing me. I said, that is right, now drive it like you stole it. She started laughing and said, you are crazy. So we drove on dirt roads for a little while and she started having fun again. I had her slide it sideways a couple times on the gravel. Then she said, alright I am not scared anymore, sliding to a stop. She pulled out the button for the air breaks, and said, your turn to drive. I said, I thought you were going to take your shirt off or something, and drive around. Laughing she said, you have weird thoughts sometimes Donnie. I said, I thought that was every truck drivers dream. So I drove us back to the house. Thanking God for helping us. (What If?)

I started back driving, and got back into the groove of it. But within my spirit I was troubled. Like a whirlwind was going on inside me. And I kept thinking dig a well. I kept giving it to God, and He kept giving it back to me. I could not go around it, or through it.

God told Abraham to dig a well, Job set on sackcloth and ash, Isaiah said, he that waits upon the Lord shall renew there strength, and mount up on wings like eagles, Solomon wrote a love letter. Some say it was to a woman, others say it was to God. And it could have been from God to us. And Jesus Christ was a man of great sorrows, that wept often. Now I don't know what is coming, so I dug a well.

I put my trust in You God, for You are the Alfa and Omega. The First and the Last. The Beginning and the End. And besides You there is nothing. I look to the East, from were my help cometh from. You are my Sunrises and Sunsets. This life I am living, I have already lived.

This went on for days, as I surrender myself and this situation to God. Then one day I came back from the wood yard at lunch time. I was asked if I would go and get the man running the chainsaw. I was told to go down the hill to the creek, turn right and I should see him. So that is what I did, the only problem was now the sound of the chainsaw, echoed on the creek. So that put me in a very dangerous position. If he was on the creek it would be fine. If he was on the hillside, the tree would fall in my direction. I walked off the creek trying to fight my way through the underbrush. When I hear the tree snap. The power of God shoved me to the left as the huge tree top fell all around me. I was now standing in the fork of the tree top. And I had to pull myself up, to get on the log part of the tree.

Now that I was standing on the log part of the tree. I could see the man running the chainsaw very clearly. As I walked down the log of the tree to were he was and said, come on we have to eat. When I said that, he passed out. I jumped off the tree trunk and fanned him with my hat. When he came too he asked, were the hell did you come from. I said, I was looking for you, its lunch time. As I was helping him up he said, you should be dead. I said, the power of God was all over me. As his legs went out from under him again. As I helped him stand again he asked, were did you come from? I said, I would tell you but you would not believe me, and we don't have that much time. So we walked up the hill, I had him by the arm in one hand, and his chainsaw in the other.

As he would catch a wobble every now and then. I said that was a very big tree you cut down. He asked, who the hell are you Donnie? I said, that would take longer to tell you, than the first question you asked me. He said, I fill sick. I said, you will be alright, you just need something to eat.

As I sat him down on a log with the rest of the men, I gave him his lunch box and some water. The other men laughing asked, if he had seen the monkey. I said, I don't think he got to hot, but he did see something. I said, it probably would not hurt anything if y'all kept an eye on him. Another man came over and set with him. My truck was loaded so I pulled my last load of the day to the woodyard, and went home.

The next morning the man running the chainsaw said, Donnie you should be dead. I have never seen nothing like that before. I smiled and asked, do you believe Jesus Christ is the Son of God? He said, I believe in God if that is what you are asking. I said, anything can be a God. That is not what I asked you. Then he said, what happened is impossible. I said, all things are possible for those that are in Jesus Christ. He looked at me smiling, shook his head and said, you should be dead. Picking up his chainsaw he said, I have to go to work. I said, Jesus Christ loves you man.

That same summer they hired another man to run a chainsaw. While he was cutting the limbs off of a tree, the chainsaw he was using was knocked out of his hands. Cutting very deeply into his right arm. Every time his heart would beat blood would shoot out of it. I grabbed a rag laying on the back of the bosses truck. And slapped it on it, praying a verse from the Bible that stops bleeding. He looked at me and said, I am going to die aren't I. I said, not on me, you are not. I got him into the truck as he was saying, I am so scared. I said, well all we are going to do is get you sewn up. Holding his arm tight he said, I have never been cut like this before, I think I almost cut my arm off. I said, you are hurt but not that bad, the blood is no longer running down your arm. He said, how is that possible? I said, Jesus Christ is on the seen.

At the hospital they came running out and took us back to a room. They took the rag off of it and stopped, looked at it, and left the room. She returned with two more nurses. They looked at his arm also and said get a doctor. The way they were acting I thought it was bad. A doctor came in looked at it, started laughed and left. Then the doctor came in to sew him up. He looked at me and said, my mom could do that. I asked, what was that? He said, pray and the bleeding would stop. Then he started washing the mans arm I brought in, he told him without a tourniquet on this, you should be dead. He worked on sewing him up for almost an hour, while he picked my brain on my walk with God.

On the way of taking the man home who's arm was cut. I talked to him about Jesus Christ. I believe the doctor and I sowed good seeds.

So dig a well if you are called to it. It may be you are a life line for others. God is my teacher, and the world is His class room. I can honestly say that the world does not hate me, but who I represent. (What If?)

My girlfriend and I moved on and now I was working in my home town. I had a run every day to the balm plant. One day my boss man asked me to run with another driver. I asked, do you mean in the same truck? He said, yes Donnie in the same truck. I laughed and said, with God and I already in the truck, it could get crowded with a third person. Laughing with fire in his eyes he said, I am sure God and you will make room for him. Laughing I said, yes sir I am sure we can. He said, meet him here at two in the morning, and do not be late. I said, yes sir. I arrived at one thirty to find the truck running with the park lights on. It was misting rain and foggy, I started walking around the truck checking it out. He said, I have already done that. I said, I do not feel good about this run. He asked, if I was sick? I said, no I am not sick, but I would feel better if you would let me drive first, or at least until day light. He said, I don't mind a bit, that will give me a chance to talk to you. I said, that will be fine. As we pulled out on the road he asked, are you a legend? I laughed and said, I am to young to be a legend. He said,they hired me to haul steel up north, and I make two trips a week. I said, I did not know that. He said, they still talk about you up there. I asked, what do they say? He laughed and said, that you can drive the hell out of one of these trucks. And from watching you they are right. I was pulling on the Interstate. I said, I just set behind the wheel God does all the driving. He said, they call you the Bandit, were did you get that c.b. handle from. I said, ever since I was a kid, it's my nickname. He said, they say drivers like you don't live very long. Y'all end up wrecking, and getting killed. I smiled and said, that is what they say.

Then he asked, do you never use the clutch? I said, I do to start off with, then I float the rest of the gears. Then I asked, you have not been driving long have you? He said, not long at all. He asked, did you drive during the teamsters strike? I said, I did. He asked what was that like? I said, a lot of wrecked trucks and dead drivers. The Country declared Martial Law and the National Guards put their vehicles on the Interstate. There were Helicopters flying close enough to you, to see in the truck. And everyone was looking down the barrel of the gun in the Helicopters. We were band to run any higher than Virginia, and across, no closer than Ohio. And that was to close for me, we all carried shot guns in our trucks. And it was a bad time for the Country. At the truck stops they would pull in wreck trucks with blood running from the doors of them. And every now and then we would run across a truck burning on the side of the Interstate.

I started to pass another truck, and the power of God rested on me. So I asked him to be quiet. It was raining and foggy. And when I checked my mirrors to come back in, the truck I was passing had disappeared. Or was he in a blind spot. I glanced in my mirrors again and then back in front of us. All I could see setting in a low spot was the back end of a trailer. I jerked the steering wheel hard to the right, and then to the left. When the truck and trailer straightened out, I slammed on breaks. He was crying, screaming and stomping the floor board. I back our truck up on the shoulder until I was beside the parked truck. He was screaming what are you doing. I said, I am fixing to set fire to that parked truck, it is the best way to let other drivers know it's setting here. I jumped out of the truck and open the side box on it. I looked under the bed of it and all that was there was a roll of paper towels. Then I said to myself, this not my tractor, I have a coca cola bottle filled with diesel fuel for such an occasion. So I grabbed the paper towels and slammed the little door. Stepping back to the drivers door I threw the paper towels to him. He was still crying and screaming, stomping again, just having a fit. I asked, who's truck is this? That's when I car pulled behind me. He said, I don't know. A man in a suit walked up behind me. I said, then there is nothing here to start a fire with. The man in the suit asked, what you boys up to. I looked at him and asked, you would not have anything to start a fire with would you. No gasoline, kerosene, or diesel fuel. He laughed and asked, what are you going to do with that driver. I realize then, I had seen him before, across a parking lot at a truck stop. This is my trouble. I said, I am going to set fire to that tractor trailer setting on the Interstate with no lights on. It's the best way I know to warn other drivers. He said, I can not let you do that, seeing it belongs to the state. Then I laughed and said, well I want you to give them good old boys, that parked it here a message. The next one I run up on, I will burn it to the ground. And I tell you something else, if you are the one that shows up at it, I will put a bullet in your stupid ass. Then I turned from him got back in the truck and left.

As I pulled back on the Interstate the other truck driver was still crying and carrying on. After some time had pasted, and he got himself back together. He said, you and I both know, there was no way for us to miss, that other tractor and trailer. Not to mention how heavy we are, and it's raining, and how fast we were going. Hell you never even hit the breaks. I smiled at him and said, there was not time for the breaks. That's the reason why I told you I just set behind the wheel. Jesus Christ does the driving. He said, I think I might be sick. I said, I feel that way sometimes. Do you still want to be a legend, I asked? He said, hell no and started crying and shaking again, blowing his noise. He said, we went through that truck and trailer. I said, well you got a reel education this morning, of what is out here. He said, if I had been driving I would have killed us both. I said, driver listen to me, out here sometimes bad things happen, and when they do, all you can do is hold on. He looked at me and asked, who are you? I said, other than a Christian, there is no correct answer for that question. I asked him, are you a Christian? He said, I am but I have never seen or been through anything like this. I said, you have entered one of the toughest life styles there are, and the tough keep going. Then he asked, are you going to pray or something. I said, I will after you go to sleep. He said, do you expect me to get some sleep. I said, not really but you could try. Then he asked, how did we do that, we did not make it around that trailer. I smiled and said, I thought you said, you are a Christian. Our Lord and Savior walked through walls, in a physical body. He busted out crying again and went into the sleeper.

I started praising and praying to God, looking at my life. Thanking God for another Beautiful Sun Rise. Looking to the East from were my Help comes from. Looking across the Mornings Sky and praying. The Eyes of the Lord Look to and fro Seeking Who He Might Make Strong On His Behalf.

My Lord and Savior, the Uncircumcised Philistine wants to take Your Land, and throw You out of it. And in prison your people Oh Lord. The Bible has not changed, only the weapons of warfare. And there is nothing new under the Son. Thank You Lord for Delivering Us out of their hands. Let there god fall on his face in Your presence, as at the temple. And let Your Joy come and be my strength. I ask now for days gone by as if they were before me. Days of Peace and Love, of Hope and Joy. I remember Lord, I remember Lord.

My prayer went on until I bumped the dock, and the other driver awoke. As he came out of the sleeper he said, tell me I had a nightmare. And everything that happened to us never happened. I said, if that was the case, I wish someone would have waken me up a long time ago. He said, truck driving was supposed to be fun. I said, I thought you knew if it shines and looks glamorous, Satan is attached to it. He asked, why do you drive knowing people are trying to kill you. I said, I have never had a job where people were not trying to kill me. I thought this is normal for a Christian. He said, if I make it back alive, I will never ride with you again. I said, you have not been out here long enough yet, to see what can happen to you.

I said, you do not understand, Jesus Christ drives the truck. He said, you act like nothing happened. I said, I could have let you drive first. He got quite and then said, I would have killed us both. I said, yes and sometimes bad shit happens. He was quite for a little while, then he asked, how close are you to God. I thought for a moment. Then I smiled and said, I feel I am not as close as I should be. But I am close enough to save our sorry asses. He laughed and I could tell he was getting better. He asked, did you know that truck was parked there? I said, no I did not. He said, you asked me to be quiet right before then, why? I said, My spirit was charged by God, I had been talking to God earlier. That is the reason I asked to drive first. He asked, are you a prophet? I said, some people say that I am. And if I am God has taught me through the Old Testament. My grandpa when I was a child said, it was a Samson Anointing. All I can tell you is this fight I am in, never ends. But I guess it is like this for all Christians. He said, I am a Christian, and believe me my life is nothing like yours. I laughed and said, when it comes to driving a truck, you have not seen enough dead folks yet. He said, not me, and I am not planning on it either. We finished our run and I never seen him again. I was told a month latter he was killed. He had ran up on a parked truck, one morning before daylight. I asked where at? I was told up north. I left the plant shortly after that.

So now I was unemployed and that put a strain on my girlfriend and I. I told her one morning after waking up, that an evangelist empire was coming to the ground. She said, that is my mom's preacher. Two months later it started to crumble. I told her know matter what happens, look at the people he reached for God. And that his season for harvest could be over. I told her even the men of the Bible ran into the same things. One prayed if only my foot steps were greased with butter like they were. When I skipped from hill top to hill top. Not long after that a psychic called me, asking me if I wanted a job. I explained to them what I have is a gift, and it is not for sale.

I moved into an apartment complex alone. I never knew loneliness could hurt so bad, as I cried out to God. But I had met a man that invited me to go camping. I agreed because were they were going, I had not been there in years. On the way there we were pulled over by Law. He looked at me setting in the back seat and smiled. I smiled back, and as the officer started talking to the driver. I started having a conversation to, but only in my head. He said, listen to what I say, and you will be alright. I thought now who is that? I tried to dismiss it, but that part of my brain would not shut off. And my since of awareness raised, as to what I might have gotten into. For the rest of the ride there, I tried to relax, but someone had me jacked up. After we arrived, we unpacked and set up our camp. I decided to walk up the road behind our campsite. And there was a man walking straight toward me. As he approached me he said, hello Donnie we got your boy last night. I said, he is not my boy, I just went camping with them. He said, well that may not be the way I see it. I said, well that is the way it is. He said, you and I will talk about this later. I said, yes sir we can. As I walked back into the camp I could tell something was bad wrong.

On the way back up the road we talked very little, but he kept glancing in the mirror every few seconds. And I felt like death warmed over. Except for the voice in my head, he kept saying. Don't say a word, look out the window, enjoy the ride. When we get you back pack your stuff, we are moving. I said in my head, I was already moving, my stuff is already packed. He said, good boy, were are we going. I said, I don't know, why don't you tell me. He said, Florida would be nice this time of year. I asked if he knew what it cost to live in Florida? He said, no. I said, I don't either. I will probably move back in with mom and dad. He said, I was thinking the same thing. I said yes. So that is what I did.

CHAPTER 21

July 29, 2021

Autobiography by Donnie Lothridge

So I moved in with mom and dad again. Dad said, he needed some help at the family business, and everything should work out great. He said let's go fishing tomorrow, it will give us a chance to talk. I said, I thought you would never asked me, to go fishing with you again. He laughed and said, you are called to the water. And it will always draw you to it. I asked how he knew that? He said, because I am, I can not stay away from water for very long, it is just something in me.

The next morning we left early. I asked why we did not take the boat? He said, we don't need it, but we are going to a lake fishing. We were quite until we arrived. He baited his hook and started fishing. I took my fishing rod, and cast it out into the water with no bait on it. As I sat down on a five gallon bucket he asked? I am scared to talk about this subject, but what is going on in your life? I said, dad that is a very serious and dangerous question. I am working narcotics, and what I don't bust I am framed with. And if I told you how it works you would think I was crazy. He asked, what are you going to do son?

I said, dad other than mom, you know me better than anyone else. And I really don't know what to do, I mean what can I do? He asked, have you ever thought about working a regular job and settling down? How about trying to raise a family? I said, I have already tried that twice dad. And both times I have been left feeling very cold. For some reason I seem to be on a journey of some kind. And from what God has shown me, I am going to the end of the rapture. I have pretty much given up on people, but not on God. And yet I love people, all I have ever done is public service. When I am in a big truck, God surrounds me, I see Gods Beauty, and Power everywhere. Until the world throws me out of it again. I guess I will become like a gypsy or something, just wondering the earth.

Dad laughed and said, I don't worry about you son, even though I do not understand you. We both know the war here on earth is between God and Satan, over men and women's souls. We both know God built cities and formed governments. And we both know Satan is a creation of God, not the creator. Only God has the power to destroy it all, and then start it back up again, like He has done in the past. And God will do it again. If you had seen what I have seen, you would understand. God only gave man enough since to destroy himself. Then God decides what we really loved.

As the sun was setting and the temperature dropped. A fog rose from the water, my dad asked if I was ready to go. I said, not yet as I wound in my fishing line. He said, son no wonder you did not catch any fish, you have no bait. I said, it was not about catching fish today. It was about being with you. Then I asked, do you feel that Spirit off the water? He said, I do, the peace and love of God. Then I remembered what God had spoken to me. I Am your teacher now, and the world is My classroom. I said, yes sir we can go home now. (What If?)

I had been at dads house for about a month, when I was invited to a Law Mans house. There were two or three cars parked in his yard. As I started to get out of my pick up truck, the Spirit rested on me. I had a flash of an Angel with a drawn sword. I thought now this is going to be interesting. As I walked in the door, there were four or five men in the house, that I knew. There were mixed drinks being fixed, and a little weed. Everything was low key, and it was normal. We talked and started playing cards. But I noticed the woman that fixed my drink put something in it. So I turned everyone in the house over to God. I became sick, and at that moment I had to throw-up. When I returned the woman that fixed my drink, and the man she was with, were arguing. They both were told to take it outside. And no one was setting at the table, so I sat at the table facing the television, in the den. I started messing with the cards that were laying on the table, thinking about God. All of sudden she comes back in the house with a gun in her hand. Walks up to the table and throws that gun in my face. She said, your name is Donnie, and I came to blow your brains out. I started smiling looking at the thirty eight, she is holding in her hand. I could see the hollow points, it was loaded with. I said, you don't know me that well, yet. And I started laughing and said, well hell you got me, a drug dealer in a Law Mans house. How many rounds you got in that revolver any way. Everyone is gathering around behind her. I said, I can see it now, the newspaper will print two people killed in a Law Mans house.

She kinda smiled and said, two people? I said, yes you don't think they are going to let you, walk out of here alive do you? I said, I have more friends in here, than you have rounds in that little pistol. But I tell you what, ant nothing happened yet. Just lay the pistol on the table, and you can walk out of here. Nobody has to get hurt or killed. She thinks about it, then she lays the pistol on the table. Pushing the people out of her way, to get to the door as she leaves.

I picked the pistol up, and took the rounds of ammunition out of it. But know one has moved, I asked, are y'all on acid or something? Then they started laughing, asking each other, did you see the Angel? Another one asked, with the drawn sword? They all started laughing, one of them said, Donnie we have told a lot of stories about you. But this one is over the top, there is no way we can tell this one. Laughing another man said, who would believe us.

That is when the door opened, it was the man that had brought the woman, that had tried to kill me. He said, Donnie, I can not leave here without that pistol, it belongs to my dad. I said, maybe you can answer a few questions for me. Like who is she, and how does she know me. Why would she poison me, and then wanted to blow my brains out.

He said, if it had been me, you know I would have done it. I said, if it had been you, I would have never given you the chance, to walk out of here. Then looking at him smiling I said, we are all going to die, it's just a matter of time, and how. I said, but we are not talking about you, but we are talking about her. You want this pistol, and I want to know what's up with her. He said, well I think she is in love with your girl. And I think your girl and that man she is living with, has taken a hit out on you. I was laughing when I asked, how much is the hit for. He said, I think he said, three thousand dollars. He said, but if they had asked me, I would have done it for nothing. I said, you are going to keep messing with me, I will shoot you with your dad's pistol. Then I said, don't she know three thousand dollars want even pay for the lawyer. Then he told me who she was, and that she was his girlfriend. I asked, where my girl was living at now? He told me, and then asked if he could have the pistol back? I said, yes of course and I thank you for the information. But the shells that go into it, I will keep. I kinda have a collection going on. He and I laughed as I passed the pistol to him. He stopped at the door, looking back he asked, how big is your collection? I said, it's bigger than you can probably imagine. He busted out laughing, as he exited the house. (What If?)

Then they said, alright now that we are all here, we can talk. They all started laughing again when one of them said, that Angel had to be at least nine feet tall. With a drawn sword, another one said. We all seen it, and we know that crazy girl, had to have seen it to. We all gathered around you to get close to the Angel. And Donnie we would not have killed her, if she would have shot you. Another one said, we might have arrested her, but not killed her. I said, thanks you guys.

Then they said, that is the reason we asked you here. I asked, what to kill me over three thousand dollars? They said, no dum ass, we had no idea this was going to happen. But as we all have seen, this is very real. We wanted to see how you were going to handle it? I said, I guess I will go by there tomorrow, and talk to her. One of them asked, are you going to kill her on a Sunday, Donnie? I said, no I am just going to talk to her. Another one said, I sure hope you can talk some since into her, if not she could get you killed. Then someone spoke up and said, I don't think she will have a problem understanding, what Donnie, will have to say. I said, she does have children, and I don't want to see her hurt, or put in jail. The man I was talking to said, shit Donnie, I think you still love her. If a woman was trying to get me killed, I don't think I would be this nice. I said, there is a lot to our story of being hurt, and she is the mother to our child. He said, I know what you are, and how you are, and smiled. Laughing I said, we need to clean this house up.

So we took all the trash and put it in the back of my truck.

We all waited until the Law Man showed up so we could speak to him. He asked, if I could be around for the next few days? I said, I could be if you needed me. But there are some things, I need to take care of first. He said, fine just don't forget me. I asked, how pressing is, what you need to see me about. He said, it will keep, go take care of your business first. I said, yes sir.

I left the next morning to go see my girl. I looked into the glove box making sure my gun was still there. As I rode down the back roads I thought. Why is this thing going crazy I am hooked to. What is up with that. As I pulled off the road on the shoulder in front of the trailer, I believe to be there's. I took the gun out of the glove box, and stuck it in the front of my pants. I walked to the back of my truck, and dropped the tail gate. Then I sat on it, and waited on someone to come out of the house. She came out of the house took about three steps towards me. Realizing it was me, she started crying and screaming. I said, know one is going to hurt you, come here and talk to me. She was still crying and screaming as she approached the truck. I said, calm down girl I only want to talk to you. She said, I am so scared, and started crying and making weird noises. I said, come and set on the tailgate of the truck, with me so we can talk. I do not wish to hurt you, I only want to ask you some questions. She jumped up and sat on the tailgate of the truck with me. And I am so scared of you. I said, you were not scared like this the last time we talked, what changed? Then she said, please Donnie I was not thinking. It was the man I live with Donnie.

I said, girl you know I was almost killed because of y'all's stupid shit. Then I asked, how much does he know about me. She said, he knows we lived in another state. But he does not know you are a Law Man. I swear it Donnie that's it. I said, I wish you would quit crying, you are making a puddle. She said, please Donnie, he will be back in just a minute, please don't hurt him. She said, for God's sake he don't even know you. I said, you don't take a contract out on someone you don't know.

About then is when he pulled into the driveway. And she started crying and screaming again. I said, I wish you would shut the hell up, so he and I could talk. He opened the car door, and started apologizing. I had know idea your name was Donnie, you have to believe me. You almost killed me the last time we met, do you remember. It was at a cocaine drop, do you remember. I said, you know my name pretty good now. He said, please Donnie I did not put the face with a name. I would have never taken a contract out on you if I had known. I asked, then who did you you think you were taking it out on. My girl slid off the tailgate of the truck, and softly grabbed my left arm. I stepped sideways pulling away from her. And said, you know better than that, don't ever touch me when I am like this.

A car pulled in with his lights on. The officer got out of the car, raised his hand for me to stop. And said, I have this stand down. I have a warrant for his arrest. My girl walked away from my truck. I raised the tailgate and left. As I looked back the officer was hooking him up.

As I left I thought how God loves us all, and how the Power of God works through us all. I thought of how the Angel of God appeared on my behalf, in front of witnesses. And what I show people is not who I am. I thought about the men in the Law Mans house. And if seeing the Angel would some how change them. Those that serve Jesus Christ, but have never had the experiences that I have. And yet I know God separated me from everything, to work with me. I missed driving a big truck, and the quite times I spent with God. And I hold nothing against no one, instead I prayed for God to help them. Some of my old friends I still think about. Especially those that told me I had a split personality. Or those that said I lived a double life. And yes I just treated my girl like my parents treat me. The things I know I am in trouble for, and need punishment. They would let me slide every time. And as scared, and heartbroken as she was, what could I do. So I prayed the prayer of protection around her, and her family. Then I thought about love, the love of Jesus Christ for everyone. The love we all should walk in.

I rode over to the Law Mans house and hung out trying to figure out this thing I was hooked to. I opened my spirit up and looked at it. I thought, is this thing trying to imitate God. It was rolling through my vision. And I felt very tired, so I took a shot glass of liquor and went to sleep.

I woke up to the sound of the Law Man crying at the table. So I walked over and asked, if there was anything I could do? He showed me the mess he had laying on the table. It was the things a person would use to shoot up with. He said, this is the reason I ask you to hang around a few days. I got this out of my sons room. I said, you know how I operate, and I am supposed to be laying low. He said, I want this son of a bitch bad Donnie. Can you get him for me? I said, I can but I will probably be put in jail with your son first. It shocked me as bad as it did him, when I said it. Then I asked again, are you sure you want to do this? You know I will burn it to the ground. He said, you don't know what this is doing to my family. And he started crying again. I said, alright give me a few days. Then he asked, how many is a few? I said, give me three days, and I will have you an answer. Then he stopped crying and smiled. I said, don't get happy yet, it will be a rough three days.

The next day his son and I got locked up. That night as I paced the floor of the jail cell, looking into the spirit realm. I said, Lord I have totally lost my mind. I am in here with an adult, that is acting like a child. Lashing out at something he can't change. And now I need your help. This is a crazy world I have stepped into. But I put my trust in You.

The Lord put me on my face in that jail cell. As He said, it is hard when we kick against the pricks of life. At that moment I took a look at my own life. And said, it is Lord, as I was applying it to every area of my life. All the violence, and hatred, the things I could have done but did not. I started thanking God for all the deliverance I had been given. That I had never gotten hung up on things, that had happened in my life. Thanking God that He always made a way for me to turn it loose. Sometimes He would just show me the monster I had become. Then I thanked God, as He showed me Saul and David. David took everything to the Lord. (What If?)

The next morning the Law Man came into the jail, and he was so mad. As he got me out of jail. Out in his car he asked me if I had anything for him? I said, no sir not yet. He said, then that is it, you did all of this for nothing. I said, I would not say it was for nothing. Your son has a serious problem eating at him. And I have one more day. He asked, do you really think you can nail these bastards in one day. I said, I still have one day. He laughed and said, I think you are crazier than my son is. I laughed and said, we will see.

The next morning I showed up at the Law Mans house, and he looked like he had not slept any. He asked, me to set down, and then if I had anything for him. I said, yes sir, but are you sure you want to do this? So I told him were and how everything was being done. He perked up and said, I can not believe that. I said, well there it is. He smiled and said, I don't know who I can get to work that. I said, oh no you know me, and don't be looking at me like that, hell I live in another state. And you know you want see me again for another two or three years. He laughed and said, alright Donnie I think I know someone that can work it. Then I asked, if that is everything? He stood up and so did I. We shook hands and I hugged him, and told him I loved him. Then he smiling and said, I don't know what I am going to do with you. I smiled and said, just love me like Jesus Christ does.

I moved to a near by town and Law Enforcement kept trying to hire me. People kept dropping hints about drug busts I was involved in. And I was seeking God, for answers.

My mom called and said, your dad's friend had passed away. And my dad had been diagnosed with cancer. She said, she could not tell him his friend had died, and asked if I could come over. I did and took him to the funeral home. On the way back home he asked me if I knew he had cancer. I said, yes mom has told me. He said, I think I can beat it. I said, Jesus Christ and you can. He kinda got agitated with me. And said, I can beat this thing. I said, dad you and I are not the same, all I am saying is you need God on your side. Then he said, they have diagnosed me with the worst kind of cancer. And it's a brain tumor, and they are talking about cobalt and radiation. I said, I have seen a few people with it. Then he asked, what would you do? I said, dad I am not you, but from what I have already seen other people go through. I said, you already know what I would do. He said, already know. You would lay before God, and say cure me or kill me. I asked, are you in any pain? He said, I am not, but I have to try to beat this thing. I said, I will back you in what ever decision you make. Because some people do beat it. But you know as well as I do what's ahead of you.

He said, in a way I feel about it the way you do. I said, well if you are going to be taking cobalt and radiation, I will find us some good Marijuana, your going to need it. He said, I thought I was going to see pink elephants the first time we smoked it. I started laughing and said, I remember. He said, you taught me a lot about it. I said, it's just medicine dad.

I did not recognize him in the hospital. He looked like a bold headed man with blue lines drawn on his head. When he got out of the hospital, I would go by and visit. He and I would watch preaching on television, and talk about God.

Mom called me one day and said, your dad would like to see you. He and I talked about salvation, and forgiveness, he was saved. Then he said, you were right I have lived these last two years, in hell, hear on earth. I said, well dad you would have never known if you did not try. He said, I wish I had died in the beginning of this thing. I said, it was not your time then dad. And it want be until you breathe your last breath. And God could still heal you. He said, they could operate again, and give me another two years. He said, but this ant living, not for me. Then he said, I am tired Donnie, and all I want to do now is go home. I said, let's just think about good things dad. Do you remember preacher Jarred, now he was a man that could make you see, what he was preaching. He smiled. Mom said, he never spoke again. Mom called me back later and I was with her, when he went home.

CHAPTER 22
The wife

I had moved in with my wife to be. And told her of my walk with God. And I felt like I was being called into the ministry. So I went to a Pastor I knew. I told him the way I was being led. As I started to leave I wished him well on his sermon. And told him what he was preaching on, was very good. He asked how I knew that. He said, we never discussed it. I said, I just do. He said, next week come and see me at the same time. And if you can tell me what my sermon is on. I will buy you the books you need. I said, thank you sir, and I will see you next week. So the next week I was there and told him what his sermon was. After he stopped laughing, he gave me a box of books. He said, I have seen God move in a lot of ways. But this is the first time, I have ever seen this. We laughed as I thanked him. And I started studying.

Her son did not like the idea of me married to his mom. He and I got into an argument over it. He said, he would never call me dad. I said, thank you I never want to take another mans place. All I want to be is your friend. Cussing me he stormed out of the house. So my wife and I, talked about her son's attitude towards me. About two or three hours later I looked at her. I said, the phone is going to ring. It will be the police, and they will have your son. She said, Lord I hope not we don't have the money for that. The phone rang and I said, pick it up it's for you. And it was the police, with her son. I said, tell them we will be right there. So she did, and as we were walking out the door. She asked, how are we going to get him out.

As we arrived the police started laughing as we shook hands. They said, Donnie we didn't know you had a boy this old. I said, well he has not realized yet, he is mine. That really started them to laughing. As they turned him over to us, I thanked them.

On the way back home my wife asked, are you law enforcement. I said, I am, I thought you knew that. The man at the pool we drink with and I, are from the same mold. She said, that is right I have forgotten. Her son from the back seat said, ant no way I am living with the police. His mom said, you will not have to worry about it. I am going to kill you when I get you home. Laughing I said, you might better wait until he sobers up. He looks like hell right now. Then I answered his statement, and said, I am not the police. And that made me laugh because of people, that has asked me if I was the police. The next morning her son came down the stairs. His mom lit into him and I stopped her. I asked if we could hear what happened. He told the story, and then said, thank you. I am starting to understand dad. I said, no not dad just friends.

After that my wife said, she would like it if we could buy a place of our own. But it had to be on the water. We started looking but lake property is not cheap. So as I was praying about it. God kept showing me something I had done as a child. There was a black and white couple that had a child. As I watched them fighting and cussing that child. I claimed the property, in Jesus Christ name. And then I told my dad, I will live right here. We were in a boat on the lake when that happened. So I told my wife, I knew were a piece of property was at on a lake. And I told her the story. She laughed and said, that is crazy. I said, but it is ours, and we bought it.

As we moved to the lake we started cleaning it up. A neighbor called to me asking. Donnie is that you? When I turned and looked it was the Law Man that I had known for years. I asked him, is that you? As we walked to each other I said I can't believe this. As we started talking, filling each other in on the past two or three years. He said, you know they almost killed me on that bust we done. I said, I heard you were in the hospital for a long time. I heard you cut a car off, that was moving at a high rate of speed. And they hit you in the drivers door. He said they did.

My wife came out of our trailer. And he asked if that was my wife? I said,it is and I introduce them. He asked her how long we had known each other. She said two years. Then he asked if we owned the property.

And we said, yes sir. Then he asked her if we were really married. She said, yes sir. He said, I can not believe it. I said, it is true, I am trying to settle down and raise a family. He asked, does she know who you are? I said, she knows some of it, and who I am with. He asked, other than the county. I said, yes sir. My wife was looking right at me. When he laughed and said, I see you kids have a lot to discuss this evening. I asked , you seem to want her to know about that. He said, Donnie she has a right to know. The things we do Donnie, will never go away. I said, well maybe I just want to live a normal life and raise a family. He could tell I was getting upset. He asked, Donnie what is normal, with a grin on his face? I started smiling to and asked, I don't know, what is normal? He busted out laughing and said, it's definitely not us Donnie. I said, well I am going to try and raise a family. Then if I have to leave I will. He said, you do some crazy shit sometimes Donnie. I said, God loves crazy people. He said, you know they almost killed me. I said, yes sir, after I heard about it, I started praying for you. He said, I thank you Donnie. I said, you are welcome, I love you. He said, I love you too. As he started to walk off I said, you know I have been killed before right. He said, I have heard. I asked if he had any Angel's in his house lately. He looked at me smiling and said, and you want to be normal. Then he walked off laughing.

The preacher

I took a job with a sand company that owned a rock quarry. I asked them who the girl was, that was found in one of there ponds. And told them what pond it was. They said, no one has been put in any of them. They were not happy with me so I left the job. In less then two weeks there was a young woman found, in the pond we had talked about.

My mom wanted us to hear the preacher. That was at the church we grew up in. He was a very powerful and anointed preacher. He said, as he was preaching. Give me three services, and if the power of God does not get a fire going. Then your wood is wet. I thought that was funny. So I thought, I will give you three services. Then my Spirit spoke and said, you will give him more than that. I said, yes sir, I will give him Wednesday night's to. So we started going to church there. As we got to know each other. He asked me to start a prison ministry. I said, yes sir, I can do that. I was already working inmates for a city I went to work for. So I started the prison ministry. I also started studying for a pastor license. Even though my calling is not a shepherd. After a few months he wanted some of the men from the church to go for a visit. It was raining and foggy that Thursday night. As we pilled into the church van. We were laughing and talking, when the power of God rested on me. So I went quite listening to the Holy Spirit. Searching to see what the Spirit was saying. I looked at the preacher and said, slow the van down. We were in a long straight stretch of road. Laughing with the men he speeded up. As we were approaching the next curve. I reached over and slapped him on the arm. I said, what ever it is, is in this curve. He slowed the van down to a crawl as we entered the curve. In the middle of the road was a car on its top, going around and around. It was dark, raining, foggy, but as the car spun on its top. We could see a woman and a child hanging upside down in the car. The preacher said, oh my God. As he called nine one one, turning the vans four ways on. We exited the van, I walked over to the other car. There was a man in it, bleeding from his nose, mouth and ears. I turned it over to God, as he came to. He said, I think I am hurt bad, is every one else alright in the other car? I said, I think they are just set still until the ambulance gets here. You may have internal injuries. We stayed until the proper authority arrived and we left.

We went on to the prison, did our visit and left. On the way back to the church, the men was all excited, about what had happened. The preacher said, Donnie would you like to explain to us. What happened on the way over here? I said, well, God showed up. He said, my mom is a prophetess, and I grew up around the prophetic. But I have never seen nothing like this. He said, Donnie that was spooky, there was no warning, or nothing. I laughed and said, I was listening, you were not. He asked, how did you know that wreck had happened. I said, I thought this was a Spirit filled church I was attending. He laughed and said, my mom is coming in to town next week. Could you meet with her? I said, I would love to.

His mom showed up, and we were at the church. As she walked through the door, I bowed to her. And said, hello mam. She thought that was funny as she said, you must be Donnie. I said, yes mam I am. She greeted her son, with a hug and kissed him. Then she said, let's set over here, and we can talk. I said, yes mam as we all set down. She said

I will start with you, looking at her son. She said, you need a whipping, and Donnie needs to have this church. I looked at the preacher and said, there is nothing like the love of a mom. And I am not a shepherd. Looking at her as the fire of God, flamed in her eyes. As she said, you are not, you are set in God. I said, yes mam I am. She said, there is a lot around you I don't understand. I said, yes mam, I don't understand it either. Then she said it again, you are set in God. Then she said, looking at her son, walk me to my car, I have a meeting to go to. I walked with them to the door and stopped. She said, hopefully I will see you again. I said, I hope so to.

As the preacher came back into the church. I asked him what his mom thought about me. He said, she had never met anyone like you. And you are set in God, for whatever it is you are to do. I said laughing, at lest it ant wild fire. Then we both said at the same time. Wild fire is better than no fire. And then we left.

The second preacher

Not long after that our preacher moved to another church. The new preacher wanted me to do an activation service. For women taking fertility drugs. I agreed and during the service I passed by his wife. And said, God has something for you to. The young preacher went off on me. As he said, you might have well told her she was going to have twins. The Holy Spirit said, as you have spoken let it be so. As I walked around the room and came back to her. He jumped up again saying the same thing. And so did the Holy Spirit. Then he looked at me puzzled and asked. That is not you talking to me is it Donnie? I said no sir, I have not said a word to you yet. He fell on his face worshiping God. All I could say is praise the Lord.

So we left the church. And a year later at a revival in another church , there he sat with a baby, in each arm. He started crying and apologizing. And I said, it's all good, just a part of God's plan. And you have been blessed. Praise the Lord.

After we left the church, we went to Brownsville Revival. And I was interested to know how God flows through other people. So I started praying for God to send me to a House of Prophets. And God did.

But things were heating up at the house, as people were cussing me, throwing there trash in my yard, shooting at me. But God kept blessing me, in the middle of the mess. As I kept praying for them. Asking God, what would you have me to do.

CHAPTER 23

Autobiography by Donnie Lothridge

Page 1 Halo Only

I went into the doctor office for a colonoscopy. And I requested not to be put to sleep. But they put me to sleep anyway. As I start to go out two men walked in, and as they are preforming the colonoscopy. They hit a spot in my colon, and they sea-sawed the instrument back and forth. Talking to me about how good it feels. Talking all there trash. That is were I believe they put the torture implant at. Then when I was getting ready to leave the doctor said. If you can tell me what happened to you back there, this one is on me. Still drowsy from the twilight shot, I said those two men that came in the room. Did some really bad things to me. It was the same two that has been with me before, when I was knocked out.

Now I had been a licensed minister for a few years. But manly I work in the prophetic. I was invited to were the leading prophets and prophetesses were going to gather. A prophetess grabbed me by the arm and said, you are with me. I want the anointing God has on you. I said, I know all gifts are transferrable but I have died before. I have been with God in Heaven, and He has shown me Hell. She said, I know but the way you flow in God, I want it. I said, God talks straight to me. I came to see in the Spirit realm to, how God flows here. From what I can see there is a big difference. She said, well I want to see, and I hope I get that chance.

After the last night of services was over she said, I did not like the way you were prophesied over. He asked you, why you gave up on an earthly dad, for a Heavenly Father, at such an early age. And he asked you, to set back down three times. Because of all you do in God. So I have three very good prophetesses that are going to tell your life. She said, just set right here, and they will come in after everyone has left. I said, yes mam, so after everyone had left they came in. They asked me where I would like to set. I said this is your Church, y'all decide were would be the best place for the reading. And then they split it up, as to how many years each one would cover. And all three would agree before they moved to the next person. And they would ask me if it was right. And they were right. The last prophetess said, you know you are hooked to the Beast? I said, yes mam I do. She said, but you are set in God, I said, yes mam I am. But when she said, Donnie please don't leave, all three started wailing. And we cried until we stopped and I asked, will God kill these uncircumcised philistines or will I. The last prophetess smiled and said, this is unbelievable. The first prophetess asked, and this is the way it has been your whole life? I said, yes mam. She said, well shit, and fell back into one of the chairs. And we all started laughing.

And then the prophetess that took me by the arm from the beginning. Stepped back into the sanctuary and asked, if we were through. And gave me another invitation to come back the following week end.

My wife and I returned and the prophetess took me by the arm again. After the service, she asked me to prophesy over the property, and tell her about growth of the church. As I opened the Spirit Realm, I told her the property was not cursed. And the growth of the church was slow, because of the platform they operate off of in God. And then God took over. I said, something is going to happen that will be heard around the world, the field of souls will turn white for four months. And then it will turn dark again. Get your people ready for the harvest. Then I said, hell your people should already be ready. And we left. She had set up camera's and lights, so it would be filmed.

Four days later, nine eleven happened, she called me on the phone asking, if I would come and teach. I said, I would love to but, I was on a course with God, even though I did not know were I was going. She said, if you ever need a job come and see me. I said, thank you very much, and I love y'all. And that was the last time we spoke.

I also went to them looking for guidance. I was fixing to move for the protection of my family. I was running with Law Enforcement and the local law enforcement was in our yard at least once a month.

As I was cutting grass with a push mower seeking God, thinking of the first prophetess. When she asked me if this is the way my life has always been? Then she said, shit and flopped into the chair. That is when someone fired a rifle at me. I never even flinched, even though the bullet was close enough to burn my neck.

I said, alright God, I will go back on the road. But let me leave a calling card first. I will leave my home to protect my family. So I called a trucking company I had worked for before. Then I called a man I knew, and asked him if we could ride together one night. He asked me who we were going to burn to the ground? I said, well they came out of a town, and got up on my back porch. And I told them then, don't say a word when I come and get up on yours. He said, I am surprised you have not shot someone. I said, so far it has not come down to me having to remove the immanent threat of danger. Oh they have given me plenty of justifiable reasons. But God keeps getting in the way. I think about there wives and children. Of course if we lived in the Old Testament, I would have a house full of concubines. Laughing he said, I don't guess they know you are a Law Enforcement. I said, I never talk about it. He said, I will be over there in a couple of nights. And you know we are talking on an unsecured line. I laughed and asked, what is that.

In a couple of days he showed up, and we road around for a little while. He asked me what I thought we were doing in Puerto Rico. I laughed and said, working on public relations of course. As we road on laughing, and talking, he asked, how hot is it were you live. I said, on any given day you can fry an egg. I said, they are using the same tactics, they would use in a city, to drive the people out of it. I said, they are forgetting one thing. He asked, what is that? I said, we are not in a city. As we road around for a little while longer he asked me what I thought about a couple. I said, I heard that to, but they don't have anything but a baby. There just a young couple trying to make it. I told him about something, and it caught his attention. He asked, why don't you come in with us. I said, I did that once, and two people are dead. He said, there are a lot of things out there about you. I laughed and said, smoke and mirrors. Were is the leak at I asked? I was just trying to live a normal life. He asked, what is that? I said, you sound like another Law Man I know, and that made him laugh. Then he asked, after this what are you going to do. I said, I am going back on the highway, but I will be around. As he dropped me off.

As I went back out on the road, I was seeking God. Asking for guidance, and protection for my family. And I knew it would not be long before I ran into my family out here again. I had pulled a few loads out of Laredo Texas, when my old family came on the c. b. A man said, hello Mr. Bandit, how are you today? I said, I am doing quite well thank you. A woman said, Mr. Bandit I thought you were dead. I said, now that ant very likely. She asked laughing, Mr. Bandit can you come out and play. I said, no mam y'all play to rough for me. Everyone was laughing and waving, as they passed. Another man said, now what you are looking at is a Pandora's Box. If we pull him out, he can never go back. I thought my cover is what they are talking about. Then I thought about the Law Enforcement I was linked to. Another group of them rode by and asked, if I would come in with them also. And that made me realize they are going to expose me here on the road. I pulled into a truck stop for fuel.

As I pulled into the truck stop to get fuel. I noticed drivers that had printed out there badges on paper. And had them taped to there windows, for everyone to see. I thought, someone is leaning hard out here. Then I started laughing and thought. If this is linked to the American Mexico Agreement, this Country really has gone down the shitter. Then I remembered what Mr. B said, I was a golden watch on a golden chain, just keeping up with time. Then I remembered, everything we have done for that Country, starting with the lets save the children program.

Then I thought, we are a Humanitarian Country, but that is from the Love of Jesus Christ. And our Constitution is based on the Ten Commandments. Then I thought, we did have prayer in school, and we had to take that out, we offended someone. We had our Ten Commandments in our Court Houses, but we offended another god. And now they want to take, In God We Trust off our money. I really wonder what God is thinking about all of this. Considering this is His Country. Now I know what some people are thinking, Israel, is God's Country. After World War One, the Jews did not have a home or Country. The United States said, according to the Bible, right here is were y'all belong. And we fought until Israel, became a Country.

Then I thought about when I died, and God took me to different places. Starting with me being on the highway to hell. And after that standing out in space, hearing the blood of the innocent, crying out to God. After that the equal rights movement, and our land being struck by diseases. Being able to hear the whole earth at one time, and understanding every person. The weed wars were next. Then God should me. I was standing outside the White House, prophesying of our coming destruction. But the last place God showed me was. What it meant to be, cast into outer darkness. Where you wish, you could die but can not. Was I watching in this place? No I was there, and the pain was for real. And when I could not take it no more, it would start all over again. It is a place without God. If you are alive on this planet. No matter how you live, or what you think your doing. The Father, Son, and Holy Spirit are with you. And when you breathe your last breath. Then it is between you and God, and what He decides will be forever. And God makes it very plan. There is only one name under Heaven given, that man kind must be saved by. And that mans name, the Son of God, is Jesus Christ.

And what you believe, you will follow, it does not mean you will be perfect. The point is not, was I slapped down. The point is how long did I stay down. And Holiness is very hard to follow. God and I have talked about that a lot. As I work my walk out with God, asking for forgiveness in Jesus Christ Name. But it starts with Jesus Christ. And the Beast is already here. So when we get through throwing God out of His own Country. And He decides His people have had enough. God will take His people to His House. Then Salvation will come, by not taking the mark of the Beast. And Satan will run the planet, with this thing called the Beast. (What If)

As I got fuel and pulled back onto the Interstate. Once in Laredo Texas, I stayed at a motel beside border patrol. The next to morning I walked past border patrol, to the cross roads.Straight across the highway was a store, that served the best food. I had walked there for breakfast. As I stood in line, to pay for my order, and a drink. I heard my name called. As I turned around, I looked at an old family member from Law Enforcement. As we shook hands I asked, what are you doing so low in the Country? He laughed and asked me, what are you doing here, is what I want to know? I said, just driving a big truck, trying to make a living. As I turned and payed for my stuff, he said, hold up, I need to talk to you. I said, alright. As he followed me out of the store he said, alright we can talk now.

I said, yes sir, what would you like to talk about. He said, I want to know what you are looking at down here. I said, I am just driving a truck, I am not looking for anything. He started laughing and asked, were are you staying? I said, at the motel beside border patrol. He asked, if I wanted to get in touch with you, can I call on you there? I said, yes sir for this weekend anyway, because I don't know were I will be next weekend. But when I am in Laredo that is were I stay. He said, that is a good place for you. I said, I think so. He said, Donnie can you try and do me a favor? I said yes sir, if I can, I will. He said, now you and I both know if you are called in on something. They want it burned to the ground. I said, yes sir, that is the way I operate. Then he asked, do you here that? I said, other than them black birds, I don't hear a thing. He and I were smiling as he said, when you leave that is what I want to hear, nothing. He said, I don't want no shootings, I don't want any killings, and I sure as hell don't want any riots.

I laughed and said, I will try to leave it the way I found it, I hope. That started him laughing as he said, you better do more than just hope. As we were laughing I said, I had some questions for you, but I have forgotten what they were. He said, they will come back to you. I asked, were is your office here in Laredo. He said, right behind this store. As we walked around the store and looked. I said, you know this is not a building, your working at an Embassy. He laughed and said, that is were you can find me. I said, thank you, and when I can think of it again, I will find you. He said, that sounds great.

I made a couple of more runs to Pennsylvania I ended up in Florida. From there I was going back to Laredo. When I got into Louisiana a black man came on the c.b. It was late at night as he said, good morning Mr. Bandit how are you. I recognize his voice as being connected to Law Enforcement. I said, I am fine sir how are you. He asked, you are Donnie? I said, I am. He asked, you were also connected with Mr. B? I said, I was. He asked, you were also given the name Golden Child? Then I thought about that for a minute. I am also a Law Man, and I am covered in this state. Then I said, now that is a name, I have not been called by in a very long time. Wondering were he was going with this I went quite. He said, you and I have got to talk, but not on the c.b. , and not now. I said, then you pick the place in daylight, somewhere like a shopping center. He said, I know what you are looking for, and that sounds good to me to. I do have to talk to you. I said, you call it then. And that was the last time I ever heard from him.

So I went on to Laredo, and pulled a couple of more loads of freight to Pennsylvania. But on the way back down the Interstate a bad spirit kept trying to get ahold of me. I asked , Father God, what is this that is trying to get a lock on me? That keeps pushing into the Spirit Realm. It is not this Halo thing, I am hooked to by the Government. They say what they have to say. Or cause me to do silly stuff, so they can all laugh. I asked, Lord God, don't they know that when they open a Spiritual door, to get to me, I can pass through it to? Then I said, this thing I am hooked to they call a Halo. In the Bible is called the Beast. And I don't think they know yet, all that can be done with it. And I do remember when I was a child being hooked to this thing. And what was done to me then. Then I laughed and said, this thing is operated like an oversized cellphone. Not in the Spirit Realm. That was before I realized they can imitate God. The Bible says, if the days were not shortened, even the Elite of God, would be fooled.

I wrestled all day with this thing, and even after I went to sleep. That night about two in the morning I set straight up in the bed. And setting in the corner of my truck. Was the man that had caused me all that trouble, for all those years. The Spirit asked him, are you a friend, or foe. Are you for us, or against us? He looked at his hands in disbelief.

And said, so this is how this works? The Spirit asked him again, a friend or foe? He just looked at hands again saying, I can not believe this. So this is how this works. The Spirit then said, in the name of Jesus Christ I cast you out. He burst into a million little lights, that flew all over the inside of the truck, lighting it up. I thanked God the Father, God the Son, and God the Holy Ghost. For my deliverance and lay back down. Little did I know, I would fight with him, most of the remaining night.

I asked God, if I could pass through the portal he came through? And destroy what was on the other side. As I did I ended up in a room in a house. There were four well dressed men setting around a table. There was a block of silver that was oblong in shape. It had a skeleton marked in it.

That's when the Angels came passed me on both sides, almost knocking me over. They fought with the demonic spirits of the house. The bar of silver was melted, and the table was turned upside down. A cross was burned into the bottom of the table. Then I asked, if I could seal up the portal the man had passed through. I was supplied with brick and mortar, that was mingled with blood. As I worked, I fought with the man that passed through it. As he would attack me with a knife, I would cut him up with the Sword of the Lord. Even after I had sealed the portal up. We fought until almost day light, and I finally defeated him.

When the sun came up I felt drained of all my energy. But my Spiritual senses was supercharger, they were looking for another fight. Now I have done a lot of Spiritual war fare in my life. But this is the first time anyone has ever materialized in my truck. Or were I had to become involved in it physically. When God would take me places and show me things. It was a lot different from this.

So I went on and dropped my trailer and picked up one going to Indiana. On the way across the Country a woman came on the c.b. She asked if my name was Donnie? I said, yes mam it is. I recognize her voice but I could not put a face with it. Then she asked, are you also known as the Bandit? I said, yes mam I am. She said, there are some people up the road that want to meet you. I said, yes mam. She said, you know them, if you are who you say you are. I said, yes mam. So I dropped my trailer in Indiana, and picked one up going up the country.

When I passed by a little store I thought, that would be a good place for me to stop. On the way back without a trailer. On the way back I got off on the exit, and looked at the little store on my left. As pulled up to the stop sign.

The woman that was talking to me earlier on the c.b.said. Turn to the right, we are to early. And there is a construction sight about a mile from here, and I would like to see there progress. I looked at the c.b. She said, you know we don't need that anymore. I can see what you see, I can hear what you hear, and I know what you are thinking. And I can even give you thoughts. I said, yes mam let's go see this construction sight. As I rode passed it slowly looking. I asked her if she would like for me to stop. She said, no but I really expected them to be farther along than this. There is a road to your right about a half mile, you can turn around there.

On the way back to the store I asked, who are you? She said, you know me, but it has been years since we last talked, have you missed me. I said, lady I don't even know you. But yes, if I knew you year's ago, I do miss you.

As I pulled into the store yard she said, park the truck and go inside. Do not be thinking right now listen. I said, well don't get me all excited. She said, they are going to take a look at you. Try not to look at them, or speak to them. They are taking a look at you. I said, yes mam. She said, I will help you out. I said, yes mam. She said, go on in the store, they are right behind you. I said, yes mam. I walk into the store and got a drink. The store door opened and she said, walk to the other side of the store. Look at the crackers and chips. I said, yes mam. As I walked passed them I kinda smiled and nodded my head. She said, good boy, they do know you. As I was picking through the crackers, each one passed by me looking. Then we all was standing around looking at each other. I was looking at the floor standing there, but I would glance up at each one of them. And there would be a picture flash of our connection. Then the boss man said, I hate to break up this family reunion, but we have to go. A ride by shooter could kill us all. We should not all be here together at one time. As they paid for their stuff I stood there, looking at them now. I wanted to hug them all, and smiled at each one as they left the store. Then I paid for my stuff. The lady talking to me said, you can leave now they have left. As I walked to my truck she said, you done good, you done real good. And you still don't remember me? I said, the only one missing is the blond. She said, I will be seeing you Donnie. I said, yes mam. I thought about the years that had passed since I last seen them. And that I would probably never see them again. Then there were other flashes of them,I was given, one at a time. And it was all good. All except for the blond I thought. Then I heard her laughing, and that made me smile.

I thanked God for them, and prayed that a hedge of protection be put around them all.

There are times in all of our lives when God sends someone special. Even if we cannot see it at the time. And even if they can not see, God is in the center of the mess. (What If?)

About two months later there were people talking about opening my Law Enforcement file. Now I already knew they had made a trash can out of it. Putting every bust they thought might get someone killed on me. They starting with the Russian mafia back in the early eighties. So after twenty years they thought, we can open this thing now, and see what we have got. So once they opened it, all hell broke loose on the Interstate, for a little while. They were fanning themselves and laughing. Then the people that knew me,that had worked with me in the past. Started trying to put the pieces together. I never pulled a trailer that did not have a company seal on it. And I never got out of route, or just hung around truck stops. Then they talk to me about being in Law Enforcement. But I was not telling them anything of any value. I thought everything they need to know about me is on this Halo. They can look at every day of life, and hear every conversation as if I was on television. I told them, when you pull this big fish up off the bottom of the river. All you are going to have is a badge.

After that they tried to stop me from going back to Laredo. They were telling me I did not have to do that anymore. And it was to close to the border. I asked, you sound like you have a lot of money, and would not mind paying my bills to? We all laughed as I passed by the rest area they were parked at. As I was almost in Laredo a travel bus passed me. As I looked over everyone on the bus was a mannequin. I started laughing and thought, now that is different. I eased over so I could look down the drivers side of the bus. A driver came on the c. b. , and asked, what are you looking at hand. I said, now that is the biggest rat trap I have ever seen. He said, that is not for you driver, that is for someone else. I said, but that sure is a lot of cheese, who ever that is for, must be important. He said, driver who ever opens that box is never going back. And it is not for you, they are going to give you amnesty. I said, that is what they keep tell me. But I thought amnesty was given to people working for our Government. Breaking laws, for the betterment of our Country. He laughed and asked, were the hell did you come from. I said, I am a Christian, and Jesus Christ put me in the world. But I keep telling Him, this is not a Monastery down here. He laughed and laughed saying, only you would come up with something like that to say. That is when he said, move on driver that is not for you. I said, ten four and rolled on. Then I thought if they are going to give me amnesty, they are going to have to try harder.

On my Halo I heard someone say, shut up stupid. And that started the laughter. Then the woman that was talking to me all across the Country said. We are going to get you amnesty, I will see to that. But there is something you will have to do for me first. I said, there is always a punch line. She laughed and said, I love you. I said, I love you too.

I picked up another load going to Pennsylvania. On the way up the road I talked to another driver, going the same way. He asked me if I knew it was military rule, out here on the highway. I said, I know that and thanked him for serving our Country. I told him I had been a pastor for many years. I asked, are you a Christian? He said, I was raised Christian, but I don't go to church anymore. And from the way I live you could not tell it. I said, well God will never give up on you. And if you wash the inside of the cup, it will show up on the outside. He laughed and said, you sound just like my mom. He said, and just like when she talks to me, I will think about it. I said, please do. I told of the Hurricane that hit Louisiana, two months before it was even sighted. I told the pastor I was under, God is fixing to give New Orleans a good washing, and He did. I also said, and if the people of Houston do not pray, they will be next. He said, that is interesting. I said, God flows through all of us, but are we listening. Peace,Love, Hope, Joy, Long Suffering, Gentleness, Kindness, and Mercy. He thanked me, and we never talked again. (What If?)

CHAPTER 24

Page 8
Autobiography by Donnie Lothridge

As I went on up the highway praising God, knowing I have never had good without evil being there. Asking God for His protection, and deliverance.

I made my delivery, and now I had an empty trailer. So waiting on my next load I pulled into a small truck stop and set there. I had been there about thirty minutes, when someone came on the c.b. radio.

They said, look who we have here, as they started talking about the loads of Marijuana they had hauled. I pushed my air brakes in and started rolling towards the exit. They asked, were are you going Mr. Bandit. I never answered them I just turned onto the road. That is when they started cussing me. So I started looking for a place to turn around.

A woman came on the c.b. she said, don't turn around Mr. Bandit they don't know you. I asked, who is this, and how did you know I was looking for a place to turn around? She said, I know you better than you think. I recognize the voice, and it belongs to a beautiful woman. I could here a mans voice I recognize to. He was cussing out everyone at the truck stop. He said, I have tried to get that man here for the past year. He finally stopped here and you ran him off. I said, I can see he has not lost his touch. She laughed and said, no and I don't think he ever will. I asked how she had been? She said, fine. I asked, what have you been up to. She said, just working, but now I have something special to do. I asked, what is that. She said, I have to get you Amnesty. I said, just knowing you are on the job makes me feel better. She said, you are just wanting to flirt. I said, somethings never change. She said, but before I can do that you have to do something. I said, I have heard that before. She said, I have to go now, but I will talk to you later Mr. Flirt. I laughed and waved at her, as she came around my truck and trailer.

My next load went to Brownsville Texas, were I was used to help move a bridge, to the lower bridge.

After that load I went to North Carolina were I was told this would probably be my new home. And that I needed a shower. I said, I might need a shower, and a safe house, but this will not be it. If they lock me down in this state, that might work. My wife, daughter and property is in close, and I can watch them form here.

My next load took me to Pennsylvania, it was unloaded and I was empty. I parked at an Oasis and slept.

The next morning I checked everything out. As I reached for the keys to start the truck I heard, do not start that truck. I leaned back in the seat and looked around. I was the only big truck there, so I reached for the keys again. He said, I told you not to crank that truck. I have been here before day light, and I have a rifle on you. I said, yes sir. He said, and I love my job. Laughing I said, I bet you do, my dad was a sniper. He said, then we have a little something in common. I said, yes sir. He said, I want to know who you are? I said, well that might take a while. I have lived a very adventurous life. He said, I am not in any hurry I have all day. And you are empty so you are not in a hurry to go anywhere either. I said, yes sir. So I told him who I was, and what I was about. He asked me some questions about my Law Enforcement activities. That I was covered under and I asked him, how he knew about it? He said, I am asking the questions not you. I said, yes sir. When it was over he said, thank you. I asked, can I leave now? He said, I am leaving you do not have to go anywhere. I said, yes sir, but you have the hair standing up, on the back of my neck. So if you don't mind I will be parking somewhere else. He laughed. And that was the last I heard from him.

As I climbed higher in the Country, I ran into an argument about me. A man said, Donnie belongs to us and he will be coming to Washington. The woman that was with the Law Enforcement said, when we are through with Donnie you are welcome to him. But right now he is going to get Amnesty. A man said, we want Donnie now. She said, no he has been working for us, and until we give him Amnesty, no one will have him. He said, Donnie you are coming with us right now to Washington D.C. She said, if you are looking for a fight you came to the right place. The beautiful woman said, like she said the only place Donnie is going is to Virginia.

Now I knew both women that was talking over everyone else. And there was a lot of people talking about were I was going. The woman that was talking to the man from Washington, she and I would fight all the time. Until I found out some things about her. And I would talk very ugly to her, and call her all kinds of bad names. But I would always ask God to forgive me. And you know what happened, I had to start praying for her. So she was fighting for me. I asked her, what should I do. She said, Donnie they can not have you until we get through. And that started another fight. The beautiful woman said, come on we are going to Virginia. I said, I can not leave her in this mess. The woman talking to Washington said, believe me Donnie I can handle this crowd. You go on and do what you have to do. The beautiful woman said, she is not alone, now let's go. So I told her goodbye and thanked her.

And down the Country we went. As we were going through Washington D.C. some old friends of mine called me on the radio. She said, do not answer them, you are to close to getting Amnesty to mess it up now. As we entered the truck stop in Virginia it was dark. My lights ran across a truck parked with two men in it. And they started talking on the c.b. about me. The beautiful lady said, now if everyone is here, we own this truck stop until this is settled. No one comes in, and no one leaves. And she took her car and blocked the entrance. I thought, well I am hear now. The truck behind me kept saying, I was a violent person. An another driver said, I can not believe I am in a truck stop surrounded by killers. I said, that is why I avoid truck stops, you never know who is sleeping beside you. The beautiful lady said, if you are scared I am sure one of these fine gentlemen, will share there bunk with you. He said, I know you are crazy now lady. He said, I was a violent person about three more times. She said, if I hear that one more time, I will turn Donnie loose on you. Now all of y'all go to sleep.

The next morning as we all awoke they processed the driver. That was scared of all of us, and he left. Then they started processing me, and the Judge was talking about busts, I had never been involved in.

Then the Halo thing kept switching my focus. And I kept looking at things I had done last week. I looked at the beautiful lady and she started her car. She was bumping the side of her head, so I knew they were messing with her Halo to. So I started my truck. And they were trying to explain it to the Judge, I did not understand. She was moving her car, so she could leave. I pulled my truck right in behind her. She said, oh, Donnie understands perfectly what is going on here, and so do I. The Judge said, Donnie you are given total and complete Amnesty over everything. As we left they were saying,I had to sign for it. The Judge said, no he does not. About a mile down the road I asked her about it. She said, no Donnie you do not have to sign for it. And you do have Amnesty. I thanked the Judge and he said, you are welcome Donnie, your Amnesty is total and complete.

As we moved on down the Interstate she said. You know he did not do you any favors. And I am very upset about them messing with us the way they did. I said, you are talking about me covering all those busts. She said, yes. I said, well it's done now, and it's covered. She said, you need to move out of the South. I said, my family is in the South. And my oath is to My God, My Country, My Family, and My State. She said, I know but I think you have given enough. And you know if he can he will hook you up. I said, I know. But what can I do but follow God. Then she said, I will see you later Donnie. I said, I hope so. And she was gone.

My daughter had been telling me things about my wife. So after leaving the trucking world. I moved to North Carolina were I could get home if I needed to. In the little town I picked to live in. I walked into the Court House. I was putting an application in with the County. As the lady took my drivers license, and started running my background. Another lady took me back through the building. Then the lady at the front caught up with us. She had my drivers license in her hand with an application. Saying you have to go to work with us. I said, mam I am trying to get a job with the County. She said, no with the police department, and I will put you in a police car. I said, mam I just came off the Interstate, I work narcotics. I have been in Virginia. I have just received total and complete Amnesty. And now you want to stick me in a police car. Are you crazy lady, at this time, that would be a death sentence. She said, Donnie we need someone like you. I said, mam I don't work close to people like that. The last time I worked close to people my cover was blown. And two people got killed, so no mam,I will not be put in a police car. She said, well the job is open if you want it. Then she looked at me smiling and asked, who got killed? I smiled and said, I am not answering that question. And all the county jobs were taken.

I did find a job on a farm. And ran into the lady from the Courthouse. I told her, I had taken a job on a farm. She said, that will keep you out of the publics eyes. But Donnie I don't know what is going to happen. I said, just keep believing in Jesus Christ, because when it's all said, and done, that's all we have. She said, I hope Jesus Christ calls us home soon. I said, it will be sooner than you think. She asked, do you think it will be in our lifetime? I said, I believe in what God has shown me. And yes mam Jesus Christ is setting on ready, and waiting on go. She said, that will be a horrible time, but a very beautiful time to. I said, yes mam I have never had good without bad, or bad without good showing up. We laughed and she left.

I noticed living off of a military post everyone was giving hand signals. And then I noticed one day they were giving my location. Then it dawned on me they are trying to hook me to this Beast thing. I said, I am already hooked to it what are you doing?

I bought a sailboat thinking, I can sleeve it in South Carolina, and my wife and I can live on it. And I took a job in South Carolina driving a dump truck. The people I would meet on the highway started begging me to go see a branch of government. So I went to talk to them. They treated me like, get away from us. That's when they turned this Beast thing on for real. Attacking me sexually with it, with great pain. Then they said, we are going to process you. This gizmo we are using on you will be turned on by some people. That will examine you, and they really want to kill you. They said, we are processing you as a pedophile. That way we can keep you hid. I said, y'all are the sickest bunch of bastards I have ever met. The man that had tried to kill me all those years, now has me. And he is not missing a chance to hurt me. They told me to lay down necked in the bed while they examined me.

As I lay there talking to them, with there gizmo they pushed against my body. Pinning me to the bed. I said, there is know need in this, I am compliant. I am in Law Enforcement and y'all are violating my rights. They said, here you have no rights. There were four of them. I asked, are y'all doctors or scientists. They said, we lean more to the doctor side. And if it were up to us, from what we have already heard from him. We should just kill you instead of going through with all of this. I asked, who made y'all Judge, Jury, and Executioner. That question caused me great pain. As they introduce themselves to me, one at a time. Then they explained to me,how this thing was going to work. They would have me at night, and the man that had in-prisoned me. Would have me during the day. He said, now what we are going to do is block your brain into four quarters. And we will view every day of your life. And I can promise you, if what we have been told is true. We will kill you on this table. I asked, do you know Jesus Christ? He said, don't ever talk to me about God. I said, I bet you, that before this is over, you will see Him. He laughed and said, why did you bring a crazy man in here. That made me laugh as I said, y'all better hold on, if you are going to view every day of my life. He said, we will see want we.

It was very painful as they quartered my mind. And as one of them started looking. He said, guys you better get in here. They came into the room, he said look. They said, that's impossible that was before he was ever born. They asked, Donnie can you remember where you were, before you were born? I said, yes sir, I was in my Father's house, running and sliding in the great halls. He asked, who were you talking to there? I said, God my Father. Then he asked, the others do you think we need to go any further. They said, yes we have to do this. I said, don't let that scare you, next you will view Angel's and a Dragon. But keep going it gets better, I have lived an exciting life. And y'all are going to view some unbelievable stuff. So they asked him if he was alright viewing me. He said, it's o.k. this is my job, so the rest of the night went well.

My kidnapper stayed that night and tortured me. He said, he did not want anyone to kill me during the night. The next day as I worked, the people on the road, were laughing and pointing. As he set my private parts ablaze. Then the people that were viewing my mind asked? Donnie have you ever been abducted by aliens? Yes sir I answered. That stopped everyone on the highway for a little while. That night they started blocking my mind again. They also started talking about God. And I started talking to them about the mind. It was a learning experience on both sides until shift change.

This man had never worked on me before, as he was looking. He said, did you know your mind is not normally. It is like one memory is scattered all over your brain. And it really is a mess. I said, I did not know that. It might be from the motorcycle wreck. He asked, what happened? I said, I died. He said, you did. I said, oh yes it is all up there. That is when he screamed and went crazy. Oh my God, Oh my God. What am I supposed to do with this. He was crying and carrying on. He called everyone to come back in and see this. I said, you found God, Heaven, and Hell. He said, now I have seen God and know he is real. I started laughing and said, God is real. Then he said, I quit I can not do this anymore. Knowing this is all real, and there is a God, what will God do to me. The visual I was given they all came back and quit. I said, wait a minute, you can not quit, this is the future. And you all now know the truth. There is one God we will all answer to. And if y'all quit who will replace you. God put a message in me for y'all to see. The Truth, no more wandering is there a God, you can now view it. Heaven and Hell, it is all there.

After everyone had left, the new man and I talked. He said, I can not do this anymore, they will just have to fire me. I said, and then what, unemployment. He said, I don't want to die, and burn in hell. I said, now that is between you and God. But let me tell you something, you are fixing to view me being interrogated, at the White House. I was already hooked up to the Beast. Before they put there torture device in my Colin. He said, you have been hooked to it, a lot longer than that. Do you remember being with Aliens? I said, I do remember. Then I said, you have spent a lot of time with someone training you, to explore the mind. And now you know the Truth, the Way, and the Life. Don't throw that away, you may need to lead someone to Jesus Christ. He said, they will fire me in the morning anyway. I have to do so much to you every night, if I work. And I can promise you, this was my first, and my last night with you. I said, do not get fired, do what you have to do to keep your job. So he did his job, torturing me. And said, I hoped you make it through this thing, and said, goodbye.

Then there was a big fight between my kidnapper, and the processors. The kidnapper left, and as I went to worked, one of the processors was with me, on the Beast.

He asked, how much do you know about what you are hooked to. I said, I don't know anything, can you educate me. He said, I find that very hard to believe, you were on a space ship. I said, oh, that. He asked, what do you remember? I said, I know this is Alien technology, and that the Alien that gave this to our Government was killed. And that they walked right passed it three times on the ship. He asked, can you tell me what it was like, being on one of there ships. I said, It was very bright and cold. They kept me on a table naked, there was a white fabric they kept over me most of the time. We passed by God's planet two or three times. They moved me from one ship to another. There was a band around my head, that control other instruments, that was used on me. We were able to talk like we do. And I was tortured like y'all do. And there were little Aliens in bubbling jars.

He said, you are right, except what you are hooked to now. The Aliens use to control prisoners with. I asked, what is my charge? He said, that is a very good question. Then I asked, if you do not find what I am accused of, will they set me free. He said, I do not know. I asked, am I in prison? He said, not yet. I asked, if this was another Country, would we not call this a coup,(koo)? And try to help them.

Then I asked, how many people in Washington is hooked to this thing? Then I asked, can another Government over take the Beast, and run our Country? Then I asked, is this the reason why President Obama was caught, flying one of our bombers deep into Russian air space? Then I said, I was told many years ago that Mexico would take this Country, and never fire a shot. Is that what this is? He said, you seem to be a man with a whole lot of questions. I asked, when I take this to Washington, do you think they will throw me off the hill again? He laughed and said, you are very funny. I said, I hope Jesus Christ comes back very soon. He said, you know more about that than I do. I said, all I can tell you is get ready. He said, until that happens you are hooked up to the Beast.

Then he asked, were God took you, at the end of you being with Him. There was nothing left in this Country, but a few people. And everything lay flat on the ground. Including Washington D.C. How do you think Satan will power the Beast then? I said, there will be enough radiation in the air to power it. I said, it is very sad, that we are throwing God out of His own Country. He asked, were is that at in the Bible? I said, King Solomon, there is nothing new under the Son. He said, when Solomon married all those wives, and let them bring their gods into his kingdom. And built temples to them. I said, now you are starting to understand. God has shown us the ending from the beginning. Then I asked, were can you find yourself at in the Bible. He said, that is not very funny. I said, I think it is, God has a special place in Hell, for those that help destroy the earth. But that is not what I was talking about. God will show you, who you are, and then rescue you. He said, now that is cool. I said, the Bible is a full life Book. And at end of our lives, we will still not understand all of its knowledge.

Then my processor said, you know I have to do so much to you. I said, that is what they tell me. He said, and I need to educate you on what to expect. I said, yes sir. He said, I can give you pain anywhere in your body. And I can mess with your mind. I can make you become addicted to the Beast. And the proper way to talk, is with your tongue stuck to the roof of your mouth. And later I will show you what it feels like, when someone is pulling information off your brain. I said, I already know what that is like. They tried to kill me with it at a truck stop. He laughed and said, I see that. I asked, why do they concentrate on my sex for. He said, that is the core of your being. He said, and you know what we have you do, for certain information. I said, I remember that even on the spaces ship, and that being done to me. He said, that was for another reason. He said, we control you through your sex. I said, well that is messed up. He said, the Bible, calls it the Beast for a reason.

I said, the Bible says, without the mark of the Beast. We cannot buy, sell, or trade anything. That it becomes our identity, it becomes us. Our doctor, our lawyer, our judge, but it is run by Satan. And that is not supposed to happen, until after the battle of Armageddon. Then there will be one world currency, the Beast. I said, and I really did not think the Beast was supposed to be here until after Armageddon. But I guess God will use it to sustain life. Then Salvation will come by not taking the mark.

I said, that reminds me, I do need to get a lawyer. They laughed and said, you can try. But I think you will found out we own them all. I said, I guess that means, you don't mind watching your brothers young daughter. Getting sodomized over at your house for Christmas. He said , I have nothing else to say. I said, with out laws put in place to protect the public, there will be no end, to what people will use this Beast for. As you know I have no defensive ground to stand on. Without Judges, and Lawyers I am helpless. And you hide behind the Constitution, for your protection, and tell me I have no Rights. I said, you are a terrorist.

Everyone was quite for some time after that.

When we started talking again, they asked if I was Mr. B son? I said, not biological. It is true, I was called his Golden Child. But that was from a prophetic stand point. They asked if I knew were a large amount of money was? I said, no sir. They said, he did leave you money. I said, he was supposed to leave me money, to fly to another country on. But it never happened. Then I asked, have y'all declared war on the United States of American? Prisoning people without a trail? They said, we are asking the questions.

I said, the Bible says, there will be one person in a household. That will take the mark of the Beast, for there families well far. Knowing that they just condemned themselves to hell. Then I asked them, what kind of lie have you been sold into? Power and Prestige, that will do you no good in Hell. Satan was cast out with one third of the Angels. So he will not need any help from you running Hell. Hell is Hot, Hotter, and Hottest. Torment, Torture, and Anguish. And the worst part of it is, you are without God. These bodies we live in has never experienced that yet. But in Hell you will, that is when you will finally wake up. And cry, Oh My God What Have I Done? But God will not hear you. In a place of Hopelessness, and Helplessness, what will you do, with no protection. Then you will see what this Beast really is.

Then they said, we are through processing you, and there is nothing here to hold you own. You are Law Enforcement with Total and Complete Amnesty. Then they got in a huge argument with my kidnappers. As they refused to turn me lose. And so they had to turned me over to them.

The rape and torture started, as they cut my teeth out, and ran me out of the state of South Carolina. I moved to North Carolina again and took a job with the county. As I looked for Federal Lawyers to take the case. The three that I seen said, we know what you are hooked too, and there is no way we will get involved. They are not hooking our family to it. As the torture was increased day and night. I said, all right this will stop one way or another. So I got out of bed one morning about three. And I drove to the federal building and set out side of it. I said, come on I have something for you. And it is not a game, like you play, torturing people.

There was another man came on the Halo and asked, is there a problem here. I said, no sir, I know who I am looking for. Then some people came out, and I was told they were part of this. I said, but they have done nothing to me. I know who hooked me up, and none of them are they. He asked, then you do know who you are looking for. I said yes sir, I drove a tractor trailer for thirty five years. And this Law officer has tried to kill me on several occasions. And now he has gained control of the Beast, I am hooked to. He asked, do you know his name, I said yes sir, but I like to call him the master of disasters. He laughed and said, carry on my brother.

So I asked, is this, what happened to the military guy that killed those people, on base in Florida? Did someone see how far they could push him? They started backing off on my torment. I sat there looking at the actions that was fixing to take place. Thinking of all the men and women that have given their lives for this Country. And why they were fighting. Then I put my truck in reverse and started going back home. As I did my kidnappers informed me, that they had sodomized me until I passed out. And they told me it could happen again. I reminded them, I know who I am looking for. And then I had the strangest thought. Other countries know they can not invade this Country physically. But what about through this thing. And then they told me that they would destroy the South first. And then take the North. What If this is a coup (koo). Governed by another Country to overthrow this one. Through our Government. I then thanked God for our Founding Fathers. George Washington said, when Tyranny becomes Law, Rebellion becomes Duty.

CHAPTER 25

Page 15
Autobiography by Donnie Lothridge

I had been hearing some very bad things, about how my wife was being treated, and her living conditions. I called my daughter, and she and I started talking about it. I said, the only thing that could be done, since I am not allowed in South Carolina right now. Is bring her to me, and we will live somehow. We will just have to believe God has a plan. So they brought her to me, and I got a job the same day in Texas. My daughter told me from all the signs, she has Alzheimer's. I asked, if she had been diagnosed with it. And she said, no but bananas is working right now. I said, alright, she and I are leaving for Texas. And I will get her to a doctor, but with me hooked to the Beast. I do not know what is going to happen. She said, well she will die if she stays in y'all's house. I said, I will deal with him later. But right now I hope Texas is still neutral in this Beast thing.

So we moved to Texas, and I got her to a doctor. He said, she has dementia, so let's put her on a good vitamin. And I was working with a man on my job, that was with the Military but was retired. So he asked me if I was alright with the Military. I said yes sir, I love the Military. He said good, we are going to stay on a Military Base for a few nights. I said yes sir. So on vacation we went to New Mexico. We seen the sights during the day, and slept on Base at night. I was still tortured during the day, and at night they would pull my brain, or halo. The first night I lay down in bed, I felt it when they connected to me. I said, I can feel that. My wife asked, you can feel what? I said, nothing I was not talking to you. And I went to sleep. This went on for three nights.

After we came back he said, give me a few days, and I might be able to tell you something. About three days later he calls me, and says the only one that can help you, will be the War Department. I said, I thank you very much. He said, I know you are going to Virginia, but they want help you. I said, that's who it started with, in the beginning. And long as they had me, none of my Constitutional Rights were violated. The sick bastards that's got me now, say I have no Rights. And this is war crimes against the United States Citizens. He said, you can try but I don't think they will see you. He said, you are going to get into trouble. I said, I already have trouble, I am looking for some relief. He laughed and said, good luck.

So from there I went to Virginia. And I got in trouble, but I got to meet with them. My wife asked, didn't you used to run with them Donnie? I said, I did but that was when they were in my back yard. Now I have done got in theirs. Then she asked, didn't you also work crowd control for the Bush campaign. I said, I did. She said, I remember that, he met us all. And kissed our baby girl. I said, he did, and our baby girl said, she would never wash that spot. Then my wife asked, are they going to lock us up? I said, they can do anything they want to do, we are in their back yard. She said, oh.

We were separated and an agent came in. They said, Donnie we can not operate on U.S.A. soil. I said, then someone else is using the same thing I have been hooked to for years against me. They said, you are going to need a senator. And go see Law Enforcement. I said, I have already seen them, and they don't want to discuss it. Then they said, get you a Senator. And that is all I can tell you. It is not us. Then I said, I know I have already been told. But I thought y'all might be able to help. They said, I hope we have told you enough to help, and smiled. I said, you have and I thank you. On the way being escorted back to my truck. I asked, will I see you at the Courthouse? They said, no, are you staying in town. I said, I wish I could but I have to get back. I have seventeen hundred miles to get back. And I am going to run my wife to Grace Land, she is an Elvis fan. And we are sleeping in my truck.

Last entry to the book!
I understand why there was such a cry in Washington D.C. For people seeking Amnesty. And our President saying he was doing his best to protect our Constitution. The Judges jobs and the Lawyers jobs.

Hooked to the Beast there are no laws, to protect the United States People. And there is no one you can go to for protection. You can be hurt or raped as much as they want to. And they can trade you, or swap you to other people. They can turn you over to the nastiest caliber of people they wish to.

Since they control you mind and your body. They can give you pain in any part of your body. From under your toe nails, to your heart. They can cut your teeth out of your head. They can hurt any vital organs they wish to.

When I was kidnapped. I went to local law enforcement. And they did not want to hear what I had to say. And if you say you hear people talking, they can put you in the county for evaluation. Maybe put you on some good drugs. And yet they put the Beast on inmates all the time. For house arrest.

From what I have seen the war is on the United States People.

I tried to get Federal Lawyers to represent me. I was told by them all. We know what they are using on you. And there is no way we are getting involved, we have families to. So I had a professional make a D.V.D. at his studio. And I gave one to every branch of Government. I have been on a Military base so they could view it. And now I have written a book.

I have watched as our Country has slowly been given away. And now our sense of morals, as our Constitution and Religious Freedoms are taken over by other gods.

And I know some of you are thinking I will shoot someone. Well believe me you want do nothing but cry. If you are hooked to this Beast. Because they can double you over in pain with it. Or kill you with it.

Since it is not run by our Constitution, who is running our Country? And what flag will we fly when y'all are through playing.

If this turns out to be a coup (koo)? What will you do. They brought the war home with them. But I am not saying nothing you have not already read.

P. S. I have total and complete Amnesty. And it will not make a difference. The Beast is replacing our Laws!

The Beast is here, and what is my charge, or crime.

With all my Love, a Patriot, Donnie Carroll Lothridge!

Lightning Source UK Ltd.
Milton Keynes UK
UKHW022111160223
417167UK00006B/136